WTF Am I Even Doing

NORMALIZING THE TRUTH THAT NOBODY ACTUALLY HAS THEIR SH*T TOGETHER (IT'S NOT JUST YOU).

Courtney St Croix & the Co-Author Team:

Ana Entera, Andrea Cox, Carly Ottaway, Jen Barnett,
Jessica Kemp, Jessica Parks, Kaitlin Wilson, Kayla Munro,
Krystal Hayden, Laura Christine Clark, Lisa Stucke,
Monika Amber, Niki Bechtloff, Rhiana Brouckxon,
Rosa Lombardi, Sandi Robertson-Brooks,
Sara Easterbrook, Shawna Kressler, & Tesha Gibbon

LEADher
PUBLISHING

Thanks so much for your support Faye!
♡ Shawna

WTF AM I EVEN DOING
Normalizing The Truth That Nobody *Actually* Has Their Sh*t Together (It's Not Just You).

WTF Am I Even Doing
2021 LeadHer Publishing

Cover Design - Courtney St Croix
Interior Design - Christina Williams
Editing - Megan Jackson and Donna Zuniga

ISBN - 978-1-7770177-8-1

For more information, visit www.lead-her.com
instagram.com/leadherpublishing
or email admin@lead-her.com

Contents

INTRODUCTION

Courtney St Croix

PHOTO: **LEAH SMITH PHOTOGRAPHY**
@LEADHER_INC
LEAD-HER.COM

Throughout my life, consistently and at various different checkpoints, I always assumed: when I finally do **X**, *then* I'll know what I'm doing. When I finally **get into first grade**, *then* I'll know what I'm doing. When I finally **graduate high school**, *then* I'll know what I'm doing. When I finally **get my degree**, *then* I'll know what I'm doing. When I finally **get my dream job**, *then* I'll know what I'm doing. When I finally **move out and get my own place**, *then, surely,* I'll know what the f*ck I'm doing. I assumed. (You know what they say when you assume).

As a human being, it's natural to think there is one magical thing that will contribute to the entirety of your success and happiness in life. It's natural because it's what we've been taught. Marketing and advertising have us believe all day, every day that there's always a product or service that will fix our problems. It's natural because we've been conditioned to believe that there's one way to go about your life, and that everybody else is doing it. It's natural because we've been shown the conventional, fairy-tale way is the only way, and that the ones who do it this way know what they're doing in life, so follow suit (or else).

When we find the right partner, we'll be whisked away and ride off into the sunset with that person and life will be grand. End credits. We're taught that if we just go to school and get educated, then we'll be able to get a job we love and live the rest of our lives working and paying for our lives and being happy without any problems. We're taught that we must get the "successful adult starter package:" a house, a car, a front lawn, a partner, a kid, and a dog. The image that was painted for me throughout my life is that once you achieve all those pre-determined things society pressures you to do...you've made it. You *know* what's up. You're killing it in the game of life. You never experience self-doubt. You don't question anything. Look at you, paying bills and grocery shopping and budgeting and commuting to work and planning your wedding and having children. You *must* know what you're doing.

Didn't our parents know what they were doing? Doesn't hitting those predetermined milestones indicate at least some semblance of confidence? Doesn't turning 25, 30, 35, 40...doesn't hitting those age levels equate to "having your life together?"

As it turns out, no. No, it does not.

When I started to realize there was a gap between how I felt I should have been functioning as an adult, and how I actually was functioning as an adult, an idea started to brew. What if...I'm not the only one who feels this way? What if...there are other people who *also*

don't know *what the f*ck* they're doing with their lives? What if...
there were more examples of people being open and vulnerable
about how they're basically just winging it? What if...we could nor-
malize the idea that basically no one knows what they're doing, and
that there's no guidebook for how to do life? Maybe we would all
feel a little better about ourselves when we view, as outsiders, our
peers, colleagues, friends and neighbors *appearing* like they have
their life together (Because we know the secret: *there is no secret.
It's anybody's best guess*).

Here's the real secret: Even if it were possible for there to be a
"guidebook for how to do life," it wouldn't be helpful. Seriously. As
humans, we are both intricately complex and ridiculously simple.
We have the ability to do incredible things with our brains, but we
like things to be simple and ordered. The world is not simple and
ordered. The world is not lived in black and white, or even shades
of grey — it's lived in the most vibrant and beautiful multidimen-
sional colour palette, with far more options than you could ever
count. No one person's path is identical or exactly replicable for
another person. There isn't one set of blueprints for every person
to follow. And yet, we like to see things categorized; we like ease
and the path of least resistance. We like to fit the square into the
square-shaped hole, and move on with our day. We like people to
pick sides and stay there, and that all-or-nothing mentality is ripping our world apart.

If there were a book on the shelf called "How To Do Life Properly,"
I'm certain many of us would buy it. If there's a shortcut, why not
take it? But it's impossible for anybody to explain, dictate or decide
how *everybody* is supposed to navigate their life. We are all *so* different. We all have different views, opinions, choices, options...we
grow up with different families, lifestyles, and distinct privileges.
How many people live on this earth? 7.8 billion-ish? That's how
many different potential paths exist. It's impossible to have just one
mapped out that you follow in order to succeed.

WTF AM I EVEN DOING is a compilation of stories from incredible women that prove this universal truth: Nobody *actually* has their sh*t together (...it's not just you). Should you feel connected to any of the authors in particular, I encourage you to reach out and connect with her to share your story. That's what this book is for. Connecting with others who have felt, or are feeling, the same way.

Nobody knows what they're doing in life, they just don't advertise that they're making like their eyeliner and winging it. You are not alone. You can do this. Whatever you're tackling in this very moment, just do your best. That's all that matters, and it's really the only thing we can do at any given moment.

Sincerely,

A fellow woman who is just winging it.

XO

CHAPTER 1

ANA ENTERA

PHOTO: @ALONAJANEPHOTOGRAPHY
@ROSEYTRANSFORMATION
ROSEYTRANSFORMATION.COM

A Journey of Single Parenthood.

It was February 2013, and after months of going back and forth, I finally asked my ex-husband if he wanted to try and work on our marriage again. We'd been separated for 10 months.

He asked if I still loved him.

I said, "Yes, I will always love you..." But he didn't mean the "you-will-always-be-the-father-of-my-children" kind of love.

So, I said, "Maybe we can start small. Date each other again while working on our marriage."

He said no.

And that day was the beginning of the many *WTF AM I EVEN DOING* moments of my single parenthood. So, you're probably wondering why I'm skipping the first 10 months, right?

Let me tell ya...

Those first 10 months were the hardest I have ever had. It was humiliating, depressing, insulting, and still haunts me even to this day. The memory of that first 10 months is hard to remember vividly, but when it comes back into focus, it never fails to make me cry...like a freaking Niagara-Falls-filling-an-Olympic-sized-swimming-pool gush of tears.

It's my children and the silent pain they went through in those first 10 months that makes me the most emotional. It's hard to rationalize our decisions and their pain. How was this all supposed to happen? Why did my children have to go through it? How can I still be a good mother after this?

All those questions...

I bet you are still wondering why I skipped that part.

It's because those first 10 months were a blur of decisions that were not thought out properly. I can always say it was my meds, but that would just be a copout. I wasn't fully there! I wasn't conscious of my actions. I just went with the flow and hoped for the best. I was hoping for a miracle — perhaps getting back with my ex-husband and going back to a loveless marriage.

My name is Ana Entera. I am a mother, a daughter, a sister, an aunt, and a friend.

For me, my WTF moments were when I knew what I was getting into, but I just didn't know how to survive it or if I even would.

But I was going to do it anyway.

#1: WTF are you doing? Hold on tighter!

That night he said no, I fully let go...of my dreams of not having a broken family, of my children not having the possibility of stepparents, of only marrying once, and of my dreams of spending my old and grey years with the only husband I had ever had.

You see, I grew up in a broken family. My childhood wasn't horrible, but my old country and customs weren't forgiving to women and children who belonged to one. Although I'm in Canada now, I am surrounded by a close-knit community from the same country. I promised myself that my children would never experience what I went through. In the last few months of my marriage, that promise was the only remaining thread that was holding me together.

I held on as long as possible. So did my ex-husband. He also didn't belong to a perfect family, but nevertheless, his parents' marriage was intact, so giving up wasn't the first option.

I said "Enough!" the first time around; he said "No" 10 months later.

We both loosened the grip on our marriage and dreams together.

#2: WTF are you going back to school for? You're old!

In May of 2013, I enrolled at Brock University for the Fall 2013 term. I was turning 36 years old, had two small children, no money, no career prospects, and was still battling my depression. I didn't even have a car.

I was so excited thinking about seeing myself walking on that stage and getting that diploma, but clearly not seeing the challenges of being a single parent and finishing up a university degree.

The first year was a rude awakening. Not only was I out of school for almost 2 decades, but there were also just too many variables I did not think of:

1. Who is going to watch my children while I'm at school?
2. How do I get to school and back on time before my kids get home?
3. What would be my major? Do I need to have a minor?
4. How can I finish 4 years of university, when according to my English TA, I don't know how to write a proper paper?
5. These kids around me are too smart, and I'm too slow.

In my second year, the flow started to feel less bumpy.

1. Most of my courses were scheduled within my kids' school hours. On school breaks, they sat inside the lecture halls with me or sat outside the seminar rooms.

2. When I studied for exams, had a group project, or did a group study, my parents would pick up my children from school. I would take a couple of bus transfers to their house, then they would drive us all home after dinner.

3. Psychology became my salvation and my focus, while I discovered an affinity for Archaeology.

4. I learned how to write a proper MLA paper and distinguished it from APA.

5. Most importantly, the younger students became my friends and are proving to be more mature than others my age.

Also, I got myself a car halfway through school, walked on stage for my diploma four years later, and my age didn't matter at all.

#3: WTF DOES CO-PARENTING EVEN MEAN? IT WON'T WORK!

The first three years of separation, we went on vacations together, celebrated birthdays together, and tackled everyday issues together.

Sure, my ex-husband didn't live with us anymore, but he came for dinner at my parents' place and went to picnics and BBQs with my family. He even spent Christmas Eve dinners with us, and we opened gifts together.

He and I also continued the birthday tradition we started for the children. Even through financial hardships over the years, we kept at it. The kids really look forward to that spinach dip and the special butter at their favorite birthday restaurant!

Of course, when they're older — my daughter will be in university when this book comes out — they might decide not to do it anymore...but I hope they know that our twice-a-year get-together was special to both their dad and me. It was a time to reconnect with my "human diary," as my daughter calls him. He always had the patience to listen to my troubles without the need to fix them; To be silent when I'm raging outwards and inwards, and just let me be. In return, he often shares family troubles with me without the fear of judgement. The familiarity, built from our years together, is a source of comfort.

My friendship with my ex-husband is pivotal. Sure, there were a few misgivings and bruised egos throughout our marriage and separation, but ultimately we decided to co-parent. We might not be good together as a married couple, but as sure as the sun comes up every morning, these two beautiful children deserve the best parents. And so, we put our best foot forward every day.

Co-parenting works for us, too.

#4: WTF are you even THINKING? Not again!

It was April of 2015. My ex-boyfriend. By some perplexing coincidences, our lives intertwined again. After 18 years, continents away, and vastly different lives lived, we reconnected.

At first, it was exciting. I mean, seriously, right?! After many years of not getting romantic attention from anyone, I was suddenly thrust into a feeling of being wanted. So, an online friendship quickly turned into a relationship. This guy wants to talk to me, laugh with me, wants to know what I'm thinking, feeling, dreaming, and to meet me again.

That last part was the scariest.

I never told him, but I was scared to see him again. The last time we saw each other, I was leaving the Philippines and migrating to Canada. I was a young, vibrant, 20-year-old then, and not the 38-year-old, tired, single mother of two kids I am now. So, I broke up with him and ended our online relationship before we could re-connect in person.

However, despite my fears, I felt I needed a break from being alone. I loved the guy, and he seemed genuinely in love with me, so why not? Fear of hurt, mistakes, and failures aside, we married in September 2016, and he moved to Canada permanently in August 2017.

Of course, the relationship has its fair share of challenges. We weren't as free of complications as we were in our teens, and it was too much to carry for both of us. There was so much going on, too much compromise, too many heartaches, too much pain, and too many sacrifices for our relationship to flourish.

He decided to move out in May 2021. As I write this part of the book, everything is still raw. Every waking moment is a reminder of the last few years of laughter and tears, of joy and pain, and of hope and disappointments. Someday it will make sense, again, and all parties will nod and say, "That's why!"

For now, I deal with it daily. I'm focusing on my children, taking all the help and support available, and looking forward to manifested blessings.

And although this risk took so much of me, there are very minimal regrets. I'm most grateful for the lessons learned and the experiences I gained. They brought me new opportunities, allowed me to meet lifelong friends, and led me to where I am today, and I wouldn't have it any other way.

Single parenthood isn't for everyone.

Nowadays, I highly discourage women who might think that if I did it, so can they. I tell them that the grass isn't always greener on the other side — that it truly isn't for the faint-hearted. No, I do not think they're weak and I'm stronger. I just have different circumstances, and my outcome is different.

My journey should not be a baseline for anyone.

With that said, I'm all for a better future. A better life. A life full of love, laughter, friendship, and occasional hiccups to make it interesting. And if a venture to single parenthood will allow the space for that to happen, then so be it.

Three generations of women in my family became single parents at one point for very different reasons. My grandmother became a widow, and my mother was left for another woman. They didn't choose to become single parents, but I did. When I said the first "Enough!" and heard the last "No," I changed the trajectory of my children's lives.

My guilt will always be there, and the doubts still come flaring occasionally. NO ONE deserves to go through the uncertainties of a failed marriage (two marriages for me), especially the children! But when I see my children now, at 18 and 16 years old, I see stronger and resilient children. Independent and smart children, with fighting spirits, kind, and more empathic to the needs of others.

Perhaps they were always like that, or they developed those qualities because of the adults' decisions. Or were they like that, and the immediate circumstances amplified the changes? Who knows?

In the end, who the fuck knows what we're doing anyway? As parents, we always strive to do what's best for our children, using the best tools available for us at that point in time. If someone tells us we didn't fight enough, they've probably never been married, nor have kids, have never loved deeply, or even lived a life past their theories and their books.

All three of us re-married; My grandmother to a kind, sweet man, and the only grandfather I knew. My mom to a strong, loving man, and the only father I truly know. And now, my children have experienced two very different types of fatherly love from the men I trusted enough to be around them 24/7.

As for me, can I still be a good mom after what happened? I'm trying every day.

CHAPTER 2

ANDREA COX

PHOTO: JENNIFER KLEMENTTI PHOTOGRAPHY
@CHEECHTHEPEACH1024
MYNDFULMOMENTS.COM

The very first thing that I want to be clear about is that I still have *WTF* moments, and I am pretty sure that I will continue to have them. We all have these moments. *WTF* is a journey of self-discovery of who we are and our ability to maneuver through these moments. I don't believe one of us is a master in this area, nor do I believe that there is a single soul on this planet that doesn't experience them. They may not be pretty or perfect — hell, they may even be downright ugly and hurtful — however, *WTF* moments are given to us to challenge us, to test our strength and resiliency, and hopefully propel us to a place of learning and growth and allow us to be our authentic selves.

I believe *WTF* moments present themselves to us uniquely depending on our life's journey and what we need to learn. I can look at my life now as a whole and be able to see the moments where I thought, *WTF am I doing?* Today, I have much more clarity that we experience EVERYTHING for a reason — yes, even the NOT SO GOOD stuff. Our *WTF* moments are gifts from the universe asking us to pay attention; to really ask ourselves, at that moment, if this is really what we want, or if we are going to continue to live our lives based on limiting beliefs in contrast from our past.

My hope for you as you read this chapter and follow my journey is that you will see the beauty in the contrast and understand that if I didn't experience these moments I wouldn't have welcomed the opportunity for growth. I am Andrea Cox, and in this chapter, I am going to share my journey with some powerful and impactful *WTF* moments in my life. It wasn't until I was ready to understand, open up, and allow clarity, vulnerability, and a readiness to accept the responsibility that I realized my life was swirling in *WTF am I doing, anyway?*

Over the past year and a half, possibly 2 years, I have decided to go down the path of self-discovery...to really find out who I am and what the last 50 years have looked like, and how that time has brought me to here and now. More importantly, I have been earnestly asking myself, *what did all those WTF moments teach me?* The common denominators that I have come up with from these moments are the lack of love for myself, clarity, self-belief, and the ability to stand up for myself and set clear healthy boundaries. I believe that if we lack in all these areas, we will continue to experience these moments until the lesson is learned and we have set ourselves on a new path.

Through this journey, I have discovered that I participated in my life from a place of self-sabotage. This place kept me safe with no accountability or responsibility. In this place, I allowed my fears and the judgment of others to decide or dictate how my life should be lived. Let me clarify that I am not blaming anyone; I am acknowledging that owning this shit is the most liberating, scary, freeing feeling a person can go through. I am ready to own my shit and say, "I participated; I gave away my power." I was a willing participant in all of it. I am owning the fact that I didn't take the steps needed to be strong enough and love myself enough to make better choices.

I have realized that other people's fear has played a huge role in where I am today. I acknowledge that I was a willing participant, but my lack of awareness of that fact makes it a huge *WTF* moment. I am also very clear that my *WTF* moments are not isolated to my home life; they appear in every single part of my life. They have shown up in the people I chose to date, the places I have worked, and the jobs I have had, right down to the atmosphere where I allowed myself to work and live. What I am getting at is that for me, it is very clear that the majority of my *WTF* moments have boiled down to my perceived lack of worthiness and my ability to stand up for myself and say that I am enough and deserve the best for myself. Our power and our growth come when we lean into these moments.

Allow me to share what I think are important and impactful **WTF** moments that I can identify as significant areas of my life that I have experienced huge **WTF's**. These areas are family, love, work, and parenting.

WTF - Family

No, I wasn't raised by June and Ward Cleaver from "Leave it to Beaver" — it wasn't picture perfect and it certainly wasn't rainbows and butterflies. Without making this story into a novel, I will say that my home life was less than ideal. As a Gen X kid, I grew up in an era where you didn't talk about certain things — you kept secrets and didn't expose or talk about what was really going on. Others might have suspected something is going on or wrong with you, but it was a time in which you just didn't involve yourself in other people's business. We lived in an era in which shame and guilt were part of who we were or what we were meant to carry alone. God bless my mom for all she did and didn't give me, as it has shaped the person I am today. However, I would be remiss to not mention that my childhood and upbringing have a lot to do with my **WTF** moments as I moved from adolescence into adulthood.

WTF - Absent Father, Relationships

I used to suck at relationships. To be honest, in every single one of my past relationships, I was looking for the love and acceptance that I missed out on from having an absent father. I was looking at my partner to fill a void that was missing in me. I was looking at my relationships as something or someone to *COMPLETE ME*. I thought that my partner would make me feel whole and that if I could just find that person, I would feel good, loved, and accepted, and everything would be fine. The most elaborate illusion I had was that I would feel safe and no longer feel the pain. *LMAO, WTF was I thinking?* How the hell could I expect others to love me for me when I didn't love myself? I was asking another person to give to me what I wasn't able to give myself, and that was LOVE. I didn't love myself enough to say *I want to love me first, and when I love me first, I will then have a partner that will love me for me and accept me exactly as I am because I love and accept myself.* The funniest part of all the relationships I have experienced is that I set them up so perfectly to share the same ending. I am not saying that the best of relationships don't experience some hardship and pain, but every single person that I would seek out would play the role of my father that I was so angry at for not being in my life. I was seeking out that pain to be played over and over again until one day I realized that they weren't the problem...I was. I'm not saying they were perfect...they came with all their own challenges and beliefs of what a relationship looked like or was supposed to be. I was looking to be saved when in reality, I am the only one that can save me. Even when I was presented with a relationship that would speak to my heart and soul and show the world I had been looking for, I walked away. I walked away out of fear of getting exactly what I wanted, out of fear of being hurt, and, more importantly, out of fear of leaving my mother (which I will get to in more detail as we move along in the chapter). How messed up is that?

As of today, I am still a work in progress and am working on loving and accepting myself for who I am — all my crazy, messed-up uniqueness that makes up me. I know that once I LOVE ME FIRST, the love I am meant to have will find me.

WTF - Work

Let's talk for a moment about how **WTF** moments played out in the workplace. I am sure you have all heard the phrases "fight or flight," "sink or swim," and "kill or be killed." I was taught that you have to work hard, and even if you aren't happy with what you are doing, you still need to keep going to be able to pay the bills (blah blah blah). *SERIOUSLY, WTF?* I know and understand that the bills need to be paid, but why was I not told that you should love what you do, find your passion and purpose, and follow your heart? Remember, I said I wasn't raised by June and Ward — and I certainly wasn't raised to feel or encouraged to pursue my dreams. *Why TF* was I not strong enough to say, *I am better than this, and I deserve more?* As life would trickle on, I would learn from the world of hard knocks.

I would find employment in places that matched what I believed about myself — environments that involved hardship and oppression. I worked in places that lacked the drive and empowerment of their employees; they were more concerned with tearing them down than building them up. The universe provided me with the environments that I "thought" I belonged in. Was it all doom and gloom? Hell no! I met some of the most beautiful, wonderful people in these places and gained incredible experiences that I may not have learned elsewhere. I have actually gained some amazing friendships from these workplaces. I can tell you, however, that I always felt like there was more for me — I wanted to work in a place that inspired their employees, empowered them to think big, aspire to be more, and engage in positive collaboration and growth. I am now on a path of finding and creating that place where I am inspired, engaged, and part of a positive, collaborative team.

WTF - Parenting

Maneuvering through the world of parenthood…without going into great detail. My mother did the best she could. I love her dearly and am incredibly grateful for all that she has given me, and I'm just as grateful for all the things that she didn't give me — it has absolutely made me who I am today. More importantly, it has made me the mother that I am today. My mother and I have shared some amazing moments together, but it wasn't until my daughter was born that I understood what was missing from our relationship.

Parenting can be tricky, and if we aren't aware of generational conditioning, limiting beliefs, we can and will pass this on to the next generation. Much of what we experience and go through stems from our childhood upbringing and can influence how we turn out as adults and parents. I love my mother, and she will be the first to admit she made mistakes — which is so incredibly brave of her to say, and yet so sad that she wasn't able to see and know her own worth.

These mistakes came at the price of her happiness and the ability to love and be vulnerable. She lost her self-worth somewhere along the way. It is hard to teach or model what you don't possess. I am not blaming or even pointing the finger at her for anything, merely explaining my experience and what I have learned from our relationship and childhood and how it has affected and relates to these moments. I wasn't taught what it meant or what it looked like to love myself or how to respect myself and others. I wasn't taught how to set healthy boundaries. I wasn't shown what healthy, loving relationships looked like. All this changed the minute my daughter was placed in my arms. She would be my most prominent teacher of all the things that my mother did not teach me.

My daughter has taught me how to love without conditions, how to love myself, and accept myself for who I am and what I have to offer. We have learned together what healthy boundaries are and what they look like. We have built this beautiful, open, honest, vulnerable relationship that I searched for my whole life with my mother, only to realize I would never find it with her. She wasn't built that way, and that is okay. My daughter has been my most prominent teacher, not only shaping me into the person that I want to be, but the mother I aspire to be. Because of her, I want to be better and do better.

As parents, our job is to teach our children to find their place in this world and create a life they can be proud of and embrace. We are meant to guide them on that journey. We should not expect our children to be the point of our own joy and happiness. We need to build and find that world for ourselves outside of being a parent. As parents, we are going to make mistakes, and that is okay. It's actually more than okay because it is through our mistakes that our kids see our humanity, strength, resilience, and ability to get up and dust ourselves off and keep going.

WTF - The Breakdown For The Breakthrough

As I asked initially, did I expect that I would come across some hard and challenging areas on this journey? Yes! Have I been getting little flickers of what was to come? Hell yes! Had I really been listening? Probably not, which totally explains why I wasn't prepared for this moment and for how hard it would hit me.

It was like I had opened the floodgates and a portal to my entire life. I couldn't breathe; I was bawling my eyes out and trying to catch my breath, sitting on the toilet with my head in my hands in the master bathroom, in utter disbelief of an epiphany I had just received. *WTF???!!!!!!!* For my ENTIRE LIFE, I have lived with my mother out of fear of the world around me, but I also recognized that she carried a fear of living alone and would say and do things to keep me in the space of feeling less than and having me believe that I wasn't capable of taking care of myself. I have never lived alone, able to be with myself in order to understand myself and all that makes up me.

I was taken back to a moment when someone asked me, "When are you going to have your own life?" I remember thinking to myself, *What an odd question for you to be asking, and really who are you to be asking me this question?* I remember responding in sort of a **WTF** tone, "What do you mean, I have a life!" **BOOM** — the light bulb went off. I now have a clear picture of why he was asking this question. It wasn't out of judgment or even insinuating that I didn't have a life. It was coming from a place of love and concern, and he could see the path I was unwilling to see. He could see that I wasn't living life for ME — the life that I wanted.

I was so afraid to embrace the world and explore my options and abilities. I got caught up in feeding my mother's fear of being alone, which kept all my fears alive in me. What an insane web to weave. On the outside, to most people, it was "admirable" that I was living with my mom. However, I gave up my power and allowed her fear to control and dictate my life. I let her fear be greater than my desire to live and explore life. I held on to a belief that I couldn't make it on my own, that I wasn't capable of doing it on my own. This was like a *WTF* bomb going off in my face, which sent me into a tailspin.

As I muddled through the explosion of what I had received and tried to pull myself together, my daughter opened the door to see the puddle of a mess I was in. She looked confused with shock, fear, and sadness on her face and closed the door. A few minutes passed, and she opened the door back up and said, *"Are you ok, mom? Is there anything I can do?"* I assured her as I was still crying and trying to catch my breath that I was good and just needed a few minutes to get myself together. She closed the door slowly again and gave me the space to pull myself together. Within about 10 minutes, I got a text message from her saying, *"I know this may not be the best time to ask this, but can we go to the mall and just hang out for a bit?"* At that moment, I decided that I needed to straighten my crown, stand tall, and step into the woman and mother I was meant to be. I am more than capable of taking care of myself, loving myself, and being the queen I was meant to be.

Sometimes, it's necessary to experience the breakdown before we experience the breakthrough.

Sometimes, we aren't self-aware enough to see what's happening in our lives isn't happening to us, but for us.

Sometimes, we need to do an inventory of the influences around us and question what feels good to us, not what feels good to others as we perpetuate their desires.

This is what I had experienced, in my epiphany moment, taking inventory of what others in my life held close in order to keep them safe, and how I played a role in that. I had to make a hard realization: we only get this one life, and we're here to live it fully expressed in our own unique way. It was time for a change, and though I didn't know WTF I was doing, it had become evident that it was time to execute even though I didn't have all the answers. That's part of the process, and what we all experience as we navigate our lives.

My journey through all these *WTF* moments has taught me to open up, allow the world in, and embrace everything that has made me who I am today, celebrating these things instead of hiding them. We are not perfect, and if we were, it would be one hell of a boring existence. Life is short. Love and embrace each moment to its fullest.

CHAPTER 3

Carly Ottaway

PHOTO: **LULA KING PHOTO & FILM**
@WEBOFWORDS_
WEBOFWORDS.CA

I force my heavy eyelids open. It's 12:47am. I have to crane my neck to look past the pile of diapers, wipes, and the bottle of Advil blocking the alarm clock on my nightstand.

I lift my baby from the bassinet beside my bed and mentally prepare myself for another hour-long feed. I do the math in my head. I'll be lucky if I get 45 minutes of sleep in before my 2-week-old wakes up once again.

I try not to think about it. Instead, I distract myself with a little game I recently started playing called *"What hurts the most?"* Is it the intense throbbing of my stitches or the lightning-sharp pain striking through my cracked nipples every time he tries to latch?

Maybe it's the burning sensation every time I go pee or the pesky knots in my shoulders from hunching over for every feed.

I'm still half asleep as I unfold the change mat on the bed beside me. You'd think this routine would be second nature by now, considering this is my second attempt. I peel off the tiny newborn diaper and reach for the wipes on my nightstand. Then I hear it. The sound of someone spraying a tarp with a hose. Except it's not a hose at all – it's a *penis*, and the tarp happens to be the patch of our king-sized duvet covering my sleeping husband's back.

Now I'm awake. I can't help myself – I laugh out loud, rushing to stop the leak and cover my baby with a cloth as my husband rolls over to see what's going on. Talk about a rude awakening. That's what he gets for having useless nipples that let him sleep through the night. Kidding...kind of.

I guess this is what it means to be a #boymom. I've changed hundreds of diapers, and yet I suddenly feel like a first-time parent all over again. A familiar phrase passes through my mind as I wrestle two wriggling and wrinkly legs in an attempt to fasten on the fresh diaper...

WTF am I even doing?

It's not the first time I've asked this question, and it certainly won't be the last.

Judging from my Instagram profile, you may think I "have it all together."

I'm happily married and a proud mom of two – a three-year-old daughter and, most recently, a son.

I run a multi-6-figure creative agency with my husband, who was my first "hire" one year after quitting my full-time job working as a senior writer for a Toronto-based digital marketing agency.

Of course, the highlight reel never tells the whole story...

To start, getting pregnant didn't come easily for me. My husband and I tried for a year before we finally saw the pink plus sign on the pregnancy test. I peed on a lot of sticks over those 12 months and experienced intense emotions as I wondered whether motherhood was even in the cards for me.

Scaling a successful business didn't happen overnight, either. I started my career in a male-dominated field, working as a young journalist for a business technology magazine. I remember crying myself to sleep the night before a big tech conference, feeling like a total imposter, and imagining what would happen if the CIOs and senior executives I was interviewing were to figure out I was a complete fraud.

Building a digital agency with my husband wasn't part of my five-year plan. I just wanted to write for a living, and I was thrilled to have the opportunity to contribute to national magazines like Zoomer, Maclean's, and Canadian Business early on in my career. The first year working for myself full-time, I had no idea what I was doing. I Googled *everything*. I may have a degree in professional writing, but when it comes to building a business as a journalist-turned-copywriter, I am completely self-taught.

Six months into growing the business on my own, I convinced my husband to quit his job and join me. That first year working together was really hard. We were officially "all in" on the business and no longer had the comfort of a steady paycheck or health benefits to lean on. There were many communication struggles and a little resentment as we learned to navigate running a business together (without harming our marriage). I questioned our naivety multiple times over, wondering *WTF are we even doing?*

But six years later, I can confidently say I have no regrets. Together, my husband and I have been able to grow our business *and* our family. Because of our partnership, I've been able to step back from the business twice for a (brief) "maternity leave." I use quotation marks because, as an entrepreneur, you don't actually get a mat leave. But thanks to the dream team we recruited over the years and the longstanding trust we built with our clients, we made it happen.

If there's one thing I've learned about myself over the last six years, it's this: if I see a glass ceiling, I'm going to shatter it.

But I didn't always feel this way...

Throughout most of my twenties, I wrestled with the idea that you have to choose between building a successful career or starting a family. I was 26 when I started my own business. At the time, I didn't know many women who had pursued a similar path: becoming an entrepreneur first, and a mother second.

Because of this, I had no idea what I was getting myself into. But it turns out being an entrepreneur teaches you a lot about becoming a mom, and you don't have to sacrifice one role in order to achieve the other.

Here are a few lessons I've discovered along the way:

1. Nothing truly prepares you for the journey ahead – no matter how many books you read or how much research you do.

Just when you think you've got it figured out, everything changes.

In business, if you're not growing, you're falling behind. You're constantly being forced to evolve and adapt. You have to get comfortable being uncomfortable and learn to embrace uncertainty.

The same goes for motherhood, and this couldn't be more apparent than making the transition from one kid to two.

The moment we brought our baby boy home from the hospital, his big sister showed him nothing but love. My husband and I were over the moon with joy. I watched our kids bond in awe, turning to my husband multiple times and saying, *"We made them. We did this."*

It turns out I've repeated similar words when it comes to our business: *"We made this. We did it."*

In the days following the birth of our second baby, I felt the dull ache of my heart swelling larger with each passing moment. I wished that along with growing a human and a whole other organ inside of me (see: placenta), I could've grown another arm or two as well.

Just like in business, I felt a constant pull to be in multiple places at once. Except instead of bending over backward for my clients, I was looking to prove to my toddler that nothing had changed – and yet, everything was different.

A few days into the postpartum journey, I remember sitting on the couch next to my daughter, with my newborn baby in my lap. I can't even recall exactly what she was doing at the time, but I gently asked her to stop. "No!" she shouted, her strong-willed personality and two-year-old tendencies shining through.

Suddenly, she pulled back her small hand and slapped me across the face with it. I was stunned. Not to mention, my hormones happened to be simultaneously dropping as fast and furious as a sky-diver leaping from a plane. I immediately burst into tears.

Leave it to your toddler to remind you what it feels like to be a beginner all over again.

It turns out that getting slapped across the face by my daughter requires a similar response to receiving negative feedback from a client. You listen to their needs and validate their emotions, you reinstate boundaries as needed, you take it as an opportunity to learn and improve, and you keep moving forward.

Perhaps, most importantly, you recognize when you need to surrender to the moment. This brings me to my next point...

2. Let go of control (You never really had any to begin with).

As a recovering perfectionist, this hasn't been easy for me. But I've realized that even when I think I have control over a situation, it's just an illusion.

I'm reminded of this fact again and again, both in motherhood and in business.

Whether you're looking to launch a new program or sleep training your baby for the first time, the approach is the same. You make a plan and set goals, but most of the time, you're just winging it. Whether you're dealing with a newborn, a toddler, or a full client roster, you never know what tomorrow will bring. I mean, who can predict a worldwide pandemic?

In March 2020, we had no idea how this virus we were hearing about would impact our small business. We braced ourselves for a hit that had the potential to be detrimental for our family. Little did we know, 2020 would end up being our best year in business to date, despite having our toddler home with us for half the year due to daycare closures.

When it comes to business and parenthood, you learn to take it one day at a time. You learn to make decisions from your gut and trust the process. You learn to practice patience, even when it feels unbearable.

Perhaps most importantly, you learn to step back, take a deep breath, and *let go.*

My first hard lesson in surrendering came when my husband and I decided we were ready to have a baby. I did everything I could to increase our chances of conceiving, starting with tracking my ovulation to get the timing just right. And yet, every month, I was filled with disappointment as I spotted the red drops in the toilet bowl.

After the birth of our baby girl, I realized the timing couldn't have been more perfect. If we hadn't been forced to wait all those months, we wouldn't have produced this perfect combination of our DNA— with equal doses of sassy and sweet—whom I hold in my arms and kiss before bed each night.

The next hard lesson came when I took my first mat leave. I had no idea how I would be able to let go of my work. But when I was enveloped by the dense fog of the fourth trimester, I had no choice. I immersed myself in the newborn bubble, trading in copy deadlines for the sweet sounds of baby coos and those heart-melting first smiles.

It turns out taking a mat leave was the best decision I could've made – for our family *and* our business. It allowed my husband and our team to step up in their roles in a whole other way. It gave me the space to ease back into work at my own pace, focusing my attention on working ON the business more often, rather than constantly working IN it.

And yet, as my due date for our second baby approached, I started facing the same fears I had the first time around. *Am I really going to be able to step back?* The business was so much bigger this time – our team had doubled in size from three to six, and our client roster (and revenue) had more than tripled. There were so many more moving parts, and it felt like there was so much more at risk.

But guess what? I did it, despite many hurdles along the way. In the weeks before our baby boy's arrival, I managed to hit all my deadlines, celebrate the 5-figure launch of my first online course, book out our services with dream clients months in advance, and hire and train a new team member. And I did most of it with a sprained ankle (that's another story for another time). Now, here I am, writing my chapter for this book less than a month after giving birth.

It's amazing what you can accomplish when you set your mind to it — when you believe in your ability to stretch far beyond your comfort zone and *make shit happen*. Growing my business and my family through a worldwide pandemic taught me just how much I am capable of. It showed me how much is possible when I'm willing to let go of control.

It reminded me that even when there's a group of people going through something similar (see: worldwide pandemic/entrepreneurship/motherhood), every individual's experience is different. This brings me to my next point...

3. Define success on your own terms, and stop comparing your path to that of the person next to you.

Imagine looking at your life through the lens of the highlight reel – the one many of us opt to share online.

What would it *feel* like?

Maybe it feels like a facade – one in which you edit out the less alluring scenes from view. It's more like a dream world than reality.

But what would it take for the dream world to *become* your reality?

What if, by seeing your life through the highlight reel, you were able to recognize the abundance that already surrounds you?

Try looking beyond the frame the next time you find yourself comparing your journey to someone else's Instagram feed.

Imagine the pile of dirty laundry in the corner of the room, placed strategically out of view. Or the toys all over the playroom. The dishes in the sink.

Just because they're not visible doesn't mean they aren't there. Maybe their path isn't so different from yours after all. Either way, there's probably so much more going on behind the scenes than you realize.

We all have our own definition of success. The problem is that we tend to get caught up in chasing someone else's, and we end up comparing our real-life experiences to their highlight reel.

Today, the success of an entrepreneur is most commonly measured in cash. We see celebrations online of $5k or $10k months. Six or seven-figure years. But we never see the full picture. We don't see what's going on beyond the frame.

And why aren't we toasting to 5-hour workdays or 4-day work-weeks? Mid-day yoga? Picking up our sick kids from school in the middle of the afternoon? Instead, we assume the need to fill our calendars to the brim in order to feel accomplished.

To me, the defining moments of success in my career haven't come from hitting financial goals, signing dream clients, or having a by-line in national publications. Don't get me wrong, I celebrate these accomplishments — but the actual moment I felt like I had "made it" was when I was able to step back from my business to focus on my family.

Being an entrepreneur has taught me that my self-worth is not de-fined by my productivity rate. This lesson has served me well in motherhood.

What's the one precious commodity you can never get enough of when you become a parent (other than sleep)? The answer is *time*.

Suddenly, your days, hours, and minutes are determined by the in-ternal clock of your newborn baby. You make plans around feeding and nap schedules. The weeks fly by, but the hours drag on.

The concept of time is the ultimate contradiction of parenthood. You find yourself counting down the minutes until the next nap, and when they're finally asleep, you end up scrolling through your camera roll, wondering where the last six months have gone.

One moment, you long to hit the pause button, and the next moment you wish you could fast forward. Don't even get me started on the desire to rewind.

You're always looking for more time with your kids and simultaneously wondering when you'll ever have time to yourself again.

Being an entrepreneur adds a whole other dimension to the equation. When you're spending time with your kids, you're thinking about work. And when you're working, you're thinking about spending time with your kids.

You suddenly recognize just how valuable *time* really is. It may not buy you a new car or a bigger house, and it can't be measured by a number in your bank account. But without it, *nothing else matters.*

The work (and the laundry) will always be there. There will always be opportunities to make more money. But you'll never get your time back.

It's through this perspective that I was able to discover what truly matters in my life. I suddenly let go of the need to be everywhere for everyone because there's *just not enough time.* Instead, I tune out the noise and focus on what truly makes me and my family happy — because at the end of the day, having the freedom to choose what I do with my time is the real definition of success.

It doesn't really matter how everyone else is spending their time; all that matters is how you're spending yours.

So the next time you ask yourself, *WTF am I even doing?* Remember that simply *doing* is more than enough. We're all figuring the rest out as we go along.

CHAPTER 4

Jen Barnett

PHOTO: **LEAH SMITH BRAND PHOTOGRAPHY**
@JENBARNETTCO
JENBARNETT.COM

S o I quit my job in the middle of a Pandemic…..
If this isn't the epitome of *WTF am I even doing,* then I don't know what is.

Now before you think, *what is this girl doing?* I didn't quit my cushy, super mundane 9-5 job to watch the Real Housewives and eat junk food all day. I started my own business to work on my terms.

I've always been someone who is on the go constantly and coming up with new and different ideas of things I want to accomplish.

For a long time, I was always looking for something more — something over and beyond the regular day-to-day grind.

I've been working in the corporate world for the last 20 years as an administrative assistant. I would go from job to job every few years because I was bored and needed a refresh. I used to feel like a failure, not wanting to stay at one place for long and losing my interest. It almost felt like I was doing something wrong.

In the last several years I have felt the fire inside myself wither away to almost nothing. My job was mundane and no longer challenged me.

It started to become mentally exhausting. Not only was I completely bored and doing nothing at work, but I was also drained and so grumpy that I started to take all that out on my family, creating an unfortunate situation at home.

The idea of a work life full of ease and fun seemed like something out of a movie, but the pull towards that desire continued to grow. It was only within the last few years that I started to believe that I could make it happen.

I started to make the conscious decision that it was time for a change, and I needed to make it no matter how hard or scary it was...because deep down, I knew I was meant for something more.

I wanted work to be in my control, not what I HAD to do to pay my bills — something I could use to achieve the dreams and desires I had for myself and my family.

I didn't know how I would get there — or what being "there" meant — but I knew a change was needed.

I'm Jen, owner and CEO of two self-made businesses.

I've been married to my teenage sweetheart for the last 12 years, and we've been together for almost 17 years. We have two amazing kids – our daughter is 9, and our son is 5. I know what you're thinking...Everyone says that about their kids, but I really am proud of who they are becoming and proud to be their mom. It doesn't help that I am super strict and make it my life's mission as a mom to make sure they don't grow up to be assholes! #kiddingnotkidding

This is my story of *WTF am I even doing* and how I came to the place I am today, as a full-on powerhouse entrepreneur working on growing my dreams while managing it one day at a time.

The journey to get to the point of quitting my full-time job wasn't something that happened overnight. Although I have a super supportive husband who encourages me to do whatever my heart desires and is always a good sport when I have a "crazy" idea, the thought of quitting my corporate job and leaving a stable paycheque, benefits, and pension was unfathomable to him at the time, and I didn't hold those feelings against him.

Don't get me wrong — the thought of quitting something stable and safe was scary as hell to me as well, and I talked myself out of it multiple times a day. I was in a constant battle with myself deciding between doing the "safe" thing or doing something for myself.

I grew up like most of my generation did: you had to know what you wanted to be when you grew up the second high school started so you could work to get that job for life.

After maternity leave with my daughter ended in 2014, I remember sitting at work and dreaming about what I could be doing, thinking of something exciting and freeing that wasn't my mundane job. I would search Pinterest all day long, looking for some inspiration and motivation.

It wasn't until 2017 that I really decided to do something. As social media started to become more and more popular, I started finding local businesses by which I was completely inspired. I loved supporting local entrepreneurs who were mostly moms working a side hustle or doing their business full-time.

I watched these women stand in their power, growing their brands and putting themselves out there.

I remember thinking, *this is it, this is what I want to do...start my own business, do something for me, and have that extra source of income for my family.*

I started to feel empowered and energized, not knowing that I was starting something amazing for myself and opening the door to my future.

I researched for months, thinking about what I wanted to create and share with my then 4-year-old daughter, who loved all things girly and pretty.

I started a product business called Phaw's Boutique *(Pronounced "Fa")* in March of 2017. I make hair ties for everyday use along with other hair accessories.

At first, my business was my escape from mom life...a place I could go to grow my creative ideas and have time for myself away from the chaos. Eventually, I started to go to vendor shows to meet and interact with other business owners. I was making new friends and doing things out of my comfort zone that I never thought I would have the power to do.

My dreams expanded more as I thought of a life in which I didn't have to work my full-time job, do something I wanted to do on a daily basis, and be financially stable on my own terms.

I eventually reached a point where I wanted to do more with my business but didn't know how to expand it. Working a full-time job and being a wife, mom, and business owner wasn't the easiest thing to manage. I knew something had to give eventually, but I didn't want to sacrifice what I wanted to do because I had too much on my plate.

I started listening to and following people within the coaching industry to help guide me through "doing it all" and being "happy." I wanted to grow my business, my "empire," but I didn't feel like it was the business idea that would get me there.

It wasn't until the beginning of 2020, when I started thinking of a new business, that things started to shift.

At this point, I was almost 5 years into my product-based business, and even though I wasn't anywhere near viral, I had a lot of social media and entrepreneur experience under my belt.

I started to see several online businesses mentioning they were needing someone to help them with administrative tasks.

With my extensive administrative background and the additional understanding of social media, I knew I had a combination of experience that would allow me to excel in this role.

This idea began to fuel my fire, and I decided to take all my knowledge and use it to help more business owners behind the scenes.

And just like that, my Virtual Assistant business was born.

I was fired up and ready to move. My husband, always so cool, calm, and collected, didn't even bat an eye when I shared my new business idea.

At the time, he definitely didn't fully understand my seriousness when I told him that this business would replace my full-time job one day.

I officially launched my business in March of 2020, before anything pandemic-wise started. I took to my product business page and shared the new venture with my supporters.

Having a face already in the online space and a group of people who knew and trusted me definitely helped my new business grow. I had people in my corner before launching.

Then the pandemic hit, and the world was in lockdown. Kids were switched to online learning, and my corporate office moved to a work-from-home format. My husband, being an essential worker, worked as he usually does.

As scary and worrisome as it was at the time, I truly believe this was a sign from the universe saying, *you have the idea, and we are giving you full support.*

I was able to manage both my business and workload in the privacy of my home and be there with the kids.

Don't think this was all sunshine and rainbows. The road to get to the place I wanted to be definitely wasn't easy. There were days that I was so overly stressed and the kids were pushing all of my buttons that I often hid in the bathroom and cried.

There really is only so much a person can do in a day, and even though moms have that superpower to go above and beyond the call of duty, it was definitely hard at times.

I was trying to build my business, but keeping on top of my full-time job made me feel resentful of all the time that it required and took away from everything else. I know what you're thinking because even as I write it, I know...it sounds like I'm a spoiled, ungrateful person complaining about my job when I was lucky to have one during the pandemic.

You have to understand that I hadn't liked my job for the last four years...I felt that it was slowly taking away a piece of me. I wanted my business to be something big, and it was so important for me to show that I could do it despite everything. This push for my business to grow was what I used to keep myself motivated, so I could get to the place I am today.

Being home made me realize how much I was missing throughout the day with the constant hustle of life. This pandemic slowdown put into perspective how I wanted our life to be.

My full breaking point was around the end of summer when I received an email from my manager out of the blue, setting up a meeting with HR and my union representative to discuss my two businesses. I knew it was serious when they mentioned both businesses by name, especially since I barely talked about them.

My heart sank, and I started to emotionally collapse into a puddle of tears anticipating what would come of this meeting. On one hand, I thought that this was the universe saying, *you want out, we are going to help you...*but on the other hand, I wasn't ready to take the leap. I hadn't reached the point I wanted to be at in my business in order to quit.

I'm a perfectionist at heart, and I needed to make sure my business was sustainable enough to show that I could do this, support our family, and not need my day job.

I wasn't mentally prepared for this push.

When it was time for the meeting, I was seriously a shaking ball of nerves, not sure what was going to happen. I assumed that with HR and my union representative both being there, I was surely going to get fired.

Thankfully the meeting was just to gather and confirm information to ensure that I wasn't operating my businesses using company resources. I was required to complete a non-disclosure form that had to be approved by our Assistant Deputy Minister. However, that meant that I was on hold for both businesses until these forms were approved, and I could not conduct any sort of business until such time.

My heart hit the floor, and it took all of my willpower not to completely lose it emotionally over the phone.

My businesses that I was trying so hard to grow were put on pause. I wasn't allowed to promote or grow my businesses, and I was shut down until further notice.

As the meeting ended, I asked how this information was brought to their attention. I was told an employee in my office personally put in an anonymous complaint to HR to indicate that I was working another business on top of my day job.

My blood was seriously boiling. Why would someone do this?

I had been working with my co-workers for the last 8 years. We had a great work vibe and really had that work family feeling down pat. It was only in the previous few years that the vibe had started to dwindle and change, making me realize how unhappy I was there.

All I could think was that this person must seriously be that jealous that I could work my day job, work on growing a business, and be home with the kids all day and still get it all done.

I was officially mentally checked out and didn't care anymore. I only gave the barest minimum I could do on a daily basis for my day job.

This new state did not help my anger and irritability when the work day was over, and I continued to take it out on my husband and kids.

My husband and I have fought more in this last year than ever before. My emotions were so high and so extreme that my intelligence was at an all-time low.

No matter how badly I wanted out of my corporate job, I needed to stay focused and stay the course to build my business after hours so I could be at a point of taking it on full-time.

There were still tons of highs and lows throughout this time. I would have a bad day at work and start to get behind on my business work, which made me feel stressed.

I didn't want to continue fighting with my husband anymore, but I was scared to keep having the same conversation, pushing in his face that I needed to quit soon. We have been through a lot together, and even though I desperately needed to do this for me, we are a team and make decisions together. I wanted him to be on the same page as me so I could make this jump and see that it was going to be ok.

It was also hard for me to share things about my business because it felt like he really didn't understand. Anything extra I was doing was putting that pressure on myself — giving me more to handle than maybe I should have had to. It was a tricky balance to manage because I wanted to show him all the good that had come from my business, but sometimes that meant I was stretching myself too thin, and I was worried that was all he would see.

I eventually started to share celebrations with him with new clients or getting paid for work I was doing so he could see my success and that I was getting somewhere with it and that my business wasn't just a hobby. He was starting to see that people wanted to work with me and have me help them grow and build their businesses together.

Around February of this year[1], I remember having a completely shitty two weeks of work and balancing my business. I was letting the resentment of having my day job take away my mental capacity and energy, and I honestly couldn't stand it anymore.

The behind the scenes corporate politics and gossip is something that I never thought was real, but it is, and I felt like our office was just going to go up in flames. Everyone was for themselves. We were no longer a team, and everyone was backstabbing each other. I mean, what kind of work life is that to endure? Especially when work is something that takes up 90% of your life? Who wants that?

---

[1] 2021

I remember being so quiet and reserved at home at that point. I was working on gaining the courage to have the conversation with my husband that I had had enough. I couldn't work there anymore.

At this point, the stay at home order had been lifted, and my parents were dying for our kids to have a sleepover at their place, so we were home on a Friday night kid-free. My husband and I ordered food to have our first quiet meal together in months, and it was silent and awkward. We both knew that a tough conversation was about to happen, and I knew that I was probably going to burst into tears just saying the words.

I don't even fully remember how we started, but the conversation flowed, and I said that I couldn't do it anymore — and he just flat out said, "Just quit."

I was in shock. Those were the words I wanted to hear, the ones I needed to hear. I needed his approval, and yet I was speechless. I had this huge speech lined up to get him to see that we would be ok, that I wouldn't let us fail.

But he surprised me, and I didn't need my well-rehearsed speech!

He has always had my back, even through all the fights and disagreements, but leaving that safety of a stable paycheck for our family is not an easy thing to do or let go of.

At this point, it wasn't about the money. It was about my mental well-being and ensuring it wasn't affecting the rest of the family like it had been for the last year.

A person can only fake being happy for so long until the anger is pushed onto the people you love the most — the ones who don't deserve it.

I can't even explain the amount of tears I cried that day. Even though we had just made a huge decision — a decision I had been wanting to make since starting my business — having it be an actual real thing scared the shit out of me.

This was finally going to be real. I was going all in on my business and had the support of my husband behind me.

I gave my corporate job 30 days' notice, and the hustle and bustle was real to get everything organized and sorted so I could leave.

For the first time, I was feeling free and not stressed.

I officially went fully into my businesses in April 2021.

On my first official day as a business owner, I was the most relaxed I had been in a long time. I was finally feeling like this weight of anger and stress was fully lifted. I actually remember having my coffee in the morning and feeling free.

I feel different...like a completely new person.

I run the day on my own terms and do work that gets me excited and is actually something I want to do. I still have days of stress or feeling "behind" on work, but the fact that I am in control of my entire day is nothing short of amazing.

Even dealing with both kids doing online learning and the chaos it brings, I feel so much better about everything. It's like the weight of life has shifted, and I can enjoy all the things. It's even becoming easier to have fun with the kids and my husband, making those great memories together as a family.

As I write this chapter, I am 3 months into the official launch of my business. There are definitely ups and downs in entrepreneurship, and I'm still working to find my groove of where I want to take my business.

Knowing that it lies in my hands is a stressful yet magical feeling. I can do anything I put my mind to. If I don't like doing something anymore, I can change my mind and work my business around, feeling good and doing what brings me joy in what I want to do.

It's not always going to be an easy road, but I know I have the skills to take myself and my business to a place farther than my dreams can imagine.

As quoted by one of my business mentors, "The sky's not even the limit." – Melanie Ann Layer

I didn't know WTF I was doing when I decided to make the leap, but I knew I had a desire to lead myself to excellence, and that's what I continue to do every day.

You don't have to know the entire route. You just need a nudge in the right direction.

CHAPTER 5

Jessica Kemp

PHOTO: **MARISSA ROBICHEAU PHOTOGRAPHY**
@IAMJESSI.K
JESSIKADVENTURES.WIXSITE.COM

When I first started thinking about what I wanted to write in my chapter, I went back and forth between motherhood struggles and work/life balance while starting a new business. These moments were definitely challenging and had me saying, "What the fuck?" often, but I think my most significant WTF moment was doing all of the above while dealing with a rare brain disorder.

Before my wedding in 2017, I was speaking to a dermatologist about clearing up my acne. As hard as I try to have an "I don't care what people think" attitude, I'm not perfect, and I struggle with body image issues daily.

From the moment I stepped foot into the dermatologist's office, I felt out of place. It looked like something out of a magazine, and I felt like I should have just placed a paper bag over my head. The doctor proceeded to tell me about different medication options, and frankly, I wasn't thrilled about any of them. I decided on the tetracycline option but was a little nervous after she described the side effects.

"These side effects are very rare, though, and I have given this medication to hundreds of patients."

Who was I not to take her recommendation? I started taking the medication, and slowly, I noticed my eyesight was getting pretty bad over the course of a month or so. I was getting frequent migraines and seeing dark spots and "twinkly lights." I remember being out for a walk with my now-husband and telling him that I could barely see in front of me because the sun was causing me to have a migraine. It was the most painful migraine I have ever experienced. I had assumed it was because of my stubbornness with wearing my eyeglasses, so I went to my local Walmart to have an eye exam and purchase a new pair of glasses. The eye doctor who assessed me said she saw something at the back of my eyes that should be seen by a specialist, and she handed me a business card with the name and number of who to contact on it.

When the specialist took a look at my eyes, there was panic in his voice. He asked me if I had been taking any medications, and I told him I had started on tetracycline for my acne. He said it had caused me to develop "pseudotumor cebrei," which is also known as a fake tumor. It mimics all the effects of a tumor without one actually being present. The acne medication basically caused the optic nerves in the back of my eyes to swell and put pressure on my brain. This condition is rare — occurring in only 1 out of 100,000 people — and to date has no known cure but various treatment options that work differently for everyone. He then proceeded to tell me that I was very lucky that I came in when I did because if I had waited any longer, I would have either had a stroke or gone blind.

I can honestly say that at this moment, as the specialist was explaining all of this, I don't even remember breathing. The urgency in his voice got worse and worse as he instructed me to stop my acne medication, then go immediately to the pharmacy downstairs and pick up a prescription. He said he was referring me to a specialist at the hospital who would soon be in contact with me. I picked up the prescription, took the dose immediately, and called my husband. As I walked out the door, it started to rain, and I couldn't help but say (out loud) "what the fuuuuuuuuuck." Of course, it had to rain...I already felt like I was in one of those depressing TV episodes, so why not add a little rain? As I hung up the phone with my husband (thinking telling him would be the hardest part), I called my mom. For anyone reading this who is a parent, I don't need to tell you the pain my mom felt as I explained to her about this rare brain disorder that I now had. For those who are not parents, imagine anyone in your life telling you this information or even finding out this information about yourself. It's confusing, scary, and honestly doesn't even sound real when you try to explain it to people.

My mom immediately flew down to Toronto from Sault Ste. Marie, Ontario (where I was born and raised) to be with me. I followed all the instructions, ate a healthy diet, and took my medication. After over a year of hard work, I went into remission. I saw my medication dose get lower and lower until finally, I broke free! Looking back, I'm not sure if I was entirely in remission or if I so badly wanted to get this thing out of my life that I convinced myself I was. I still had to go back for monthly visits, but they were very short. In fact, they were so short they started to become just an annoyance for me. *I'm better. I don't have to be here,* I thought.

In January 2019, I found out I was pregnant. My anxiety was through the roof. I had planned motherhood out in my head. I worked for years with kids of various ages in child care, and I was ready to be pregnant…or so I thought. The instant I found out, I remember messaging one of my best friends because my husband was already at work. We were so happy, but as I was getting ready to go to work myself, I remember thinking, *okay, now what? I'm pregnant, what am I supposed to do?* I grabbed my stomach and walked around the apartment like a penguin because I was scared to move or do anything that would hurt the baby. I quickly realized that I couldn't walk in public like that because it looked like I pooped my pants, so I took some calming breaths and headed to the subway station.

Over the course of my pregnancy, I followed up with my specialist and my OB/GYN regularly. Near the end of my pregnancy, it was summertime (I know, right? The worst when you're pregnant!). I had gone on maternity leave early because heat + full-time job looking after 15 toddlers + Lord only knows how many extra pounds I was carrying around = torture! On top of all of that, little did I know I was suffering from gallstones, which got misdiagnosed in my pregnancy as "it's your first baby, you just never experienced the cramping before." Even a friend (who is no longer a friend) at the time said, "You really need to calm down. Stress isn't good for the baby." For context, she said this after I told her my husband heard me screaming down the hall of our apartment complex and had to call 9-1-1. Great response from a friend, right?

Well, once my daughter was born, that pain got worse, and I knew something was wrong. I pushed for answers, and it turns out I was right! I had gallstones and needed to have my gallbladder removed. My gallbladder surgery brought us into 2020, which, as we know, was the year *everyone* was saying, "WTF AM I EVEN DOING?" Just like many others during the pandemic, I felt the need to chase after my childhood dreams and started my own business as a writer/author. I published my very first children's book (that whole experience from start to finish was a WTF moment) and very slowly started getting headaches or blurry vision again, but I assumed they were caused by the stress of being a new mom, starting a new business, and self-publishing my own book. Spoiler alert: It wasn't!

Starting a new business with a new baby wasn't easy, and obviously, I wasn't going to turn into a bestselling children's author overnight. As hard as I tried, I honestly had no idea *what the fuck* I was doing. How was I supposed to get clients? How do I price my services? How do I describe my business? Who is going to buy my books? Who will hire me as a writer? WHAT THE FUCK AM I EVEN DOING??

In February of 2021 I started working at a child care centre that can only be described as heaven on earth. I knew I had to return to work full-time because we were barely making it on the little money I was bringing in. Once I paid for the cost of publishing my book, there was really nothing left over. This job came at a perfect time, and it was a wonderful blend of my two career loves — caring for children and writing. My boss was kind enough to allow my books to be put on the shelves in each classroom, and I was also able to give them out to the parents in my room as a gift.

Almost immediately after starting my job, I noticed my symptoms getting worse. I made an appointment with my specialist (whom I hadn't seen in nearly a year due to my gallbladder surgery, then getting thrown into the COVID-19 pandemic). Again, I was the queen of denial and just assumed that my new full-time job taking care of toddlers + running a struggling business + being a mom + being a wife ran my body into the ground, and I just needed more sleep.

After a few checkups (in one of which I was told my IIH had returned) and a very scary MRI (I completely forgot how suffocating they are), I sat in one of the doctors' rooms waiting to hear my results. When the door opened, four people walked through — two specialists and two residents. My heart dropped, my face went red, and I wanted to cry…but I couldn't. They explained that the blood wasn't draining properly from my brain, and the only solution was to have a stent placed in my brain.

So much for a bit of background info, right? But hey, at least you are all caught up. As the date to leave work for my sick leave approaches, I am finding it more difficult to make it through the day. I spent so much time being in denial of my condition that when I found out it came back I didn't know what to do. I remember when I first found out, and one of my best friends told me about online support groups. That alone was shocking because I didn't think I needed one, but what really freaked me out was when I found a support group, I realized my condition had its own ribbon and its own Find a Cure movement. I didn't even know what to do with myself. How could this actually be happening? That has been the only thing I can think about lately. **Why is it that it takes something awful to happen before we realize that life is too short?** I have so many dreams with my business, like creating many more children's books, but after working with toddlers all day and coming home to my own toddler, all I want to do is take a nap. I keep questioning my decision to start my own company because, honestly, it seems like some days I couldn't keep my shit together if I tried. I can't help but see other people's businesses do so well, and I think, "WTF AM I EVEN DOING?"

I don't know the first thing about running a business. I have just enough money to pay bills every month, student loan debt knocking at my door, a very active toddler, a marriage that unfortunately gets put on the back burner too frequently, and a diagnosis that I can no longer run from. I feel like every time I make some progress in my business, I get thrown off course. This illness is taking a toll on me physically and mentally. I feel guilty calling in sick even though I have a wonderfully supportive employer, and I feel like every day I don't go into work, I let my coworkers down even though my team has given me nothing but love since day one. The worst feeling in the world is being so drained on the weekends that I can't be there 100% for my daughter. It is the absolute worst mom guilt. I remember hiding away in my shower before heading off to work and just crying. Do I really think I'll be a successful author one day? How can that happen when I'm working full-time, being a full-time mom, and managing an illness that I'll have for the rest of my life? Not to mention my wonderful husband, who gets pushed to the bottom of my list because everything else seems to come first.

Social media makes it easy to manipulate others into believing that everything is simple and perfect. It's not realistic. I may not know what I'm doing when it comes to my business or my health, and guess what? Sometimes I don't even know what I'm doing as a parent! But that's okay, I'm trying my best. I'm not perfect, I make mistakes, and I'm going to fail sometimes, but one thing for sure is that I'm not going to give up. I want to inspire others with my writing, and I want to spread love, diversity, and kindness through it. I want to be in a successful place in life where I can use my money to help make a difference in this world. I have absolutely no idea how I will do it. I don't even know if anyone will care, but I want to try and make this dream a reality. I want to fight through this illness until one day I hear the word "remission" again.

Clearly, I want to do a lot of things and plan to, but so should you. **Don't let fear stop you from doing something because you have no idea how the fuck to do it.** Just start, take that first step, because the truth is no one really knows what the fuck they are doing sometimes, and who decided we had to have all the answers?

I don't have all the answers, I don't need all the answers, and I don't want all the answers. Sometimes you need to scream from the rooftops, "WHAT THE FUCK AM I EVEN DOING?"

Trust me. It's fun!

CHAPTER 6

Jessica Parks

@JEASPA

I could say this journey began on October 6, 2019. In actuality, I believe it all began January 30, 2019 — the day I found out I was pregnant. Eleven pregnancy tests, one round of bloodwork, and an ultrasound confirmed it; I was 6 weeks pregnant, nervous, scared, and worried, but over-the-moon excited. As a first-time mother, I did ALL the research, joined Facebook groups for moms, read books, consulted Dr. Google, went to birthing classes — I looked at and did it all. I thought I had learned all I could. Boy, was I wrong!

The entire pregnancy was going smoothly, and I had heard people talk about how they felt their baby's hiccups and watched the baby's tiny hands and feet run across their belly. I kept to myself the entire forty weeks that I never got to experience any of this. Four days before my due date, my fiancé and I attended one of my last OB appointments. She asked her routine questions that were followed up with the "normal" answers. Then she asked the question I was dreading: "When was the last time you felt the baby move?" I then had to stop and think and honestly could not remember the last time that I had really felt the baby move. She then listened for the baby's heartbeat, and I swear it was less than a second later that she was telling me and my fiancé to get to the hospital for a check-up. As I called my parents and let them know what was going on, more fear sunk in. Away to the hospital we went, and I was hooked up to a machine to monitor the baby's movements. Everything came back normal, and we went home without giving it a second thought.

Later that week, my due date came and went, and I found myself a week overdue. During that time, I got all the questions thrown at me: "You must be so done!" "Aren't you sick of being pregnant?" and the infamous, "You're still pregnant?!" Against everyone's beliefs, I was fine. Even though I did try every trick in the book to make her come, she was just not ready to make her appearance. I started my maternity leave the week before my due date...joke's on me that it turned out to be two weeks. In the long run, it was probably a blessing in disguise. You see, I am not the type of person that likes to sit still for too long, so that "last week" I thought I had before my due date, I was in full-blown nesting mode. My apartment was so clean you could have eaten off the floors. With my due date in the rearview mirror, all that came was a clean apartment and a whole lot more free time. Thank you, Netflix, for providing all the Grey's Anatomy one person needs.

My induction date was quickly approaching, and with nothing working to get this baby out of me, it looked like I was going to be induced. I had heard horror stories from other moms about how it is the absolute worst way you can go into labour because it is not "natural." But with no other option, it had to be done, so away to the hospital we went. I once again found myself lying in the same triage bed where I had just been not even a week prior, with the same routine: hook me up, press the button when I feel movement, and periodical checks by the world's sweetest nurse. Only a short twenty minutes later, she came back and asked, "How was that one?" "How was that one, what?" I replied. She confirmed I was having contractions about every 2 minutes. I was in utter disbelief! The nurse called the doctor to make sure it was still okay to go ahead with being induced since I was not far enough along in natural labor to be admitted at that point. The nurse received the all-clear, and, well...I will save you from the next part. I was sent home drugged up on some sort of pain killer and with a list of instructions. One of those instructions was to come back to the hospital later that night at 8:00 PM if nothing had changed. Well, by 3:00 PM, this baby girl had made up her mind it was time to come, and for what seemed like the millionth time went back to the hospital, back to that same triage bed to be assessed. Skip ahead a few hours, one epidural, one round of Pitocin, some puking, and sixteen minutes of pushing, and she was here. At 12:31 AM, the cutest baby in the entire world was born (I may be a little biased). After that, things were a complete blur until the nurse said, "She's hungry; it's time to feed her." Being a first-time mom and having only "practiced" techniques on a rubber ball in birthing class, I was CLUELESS as to what to do next. How the hell was I supposed to know what to do? And then she LEFT the room! Can you believe it? She just left?! I was in shock. Left?! Who is she?! She came back a few minutes later to help, but I still felt useless.

After a little while had passed, my family came back into the room to meet our newest addition, Parker. They took their pictures, got their snuggles, and then went home. It was just my fiancé Nolan, Parker, the nurse, and I left in the room. The nurse weighed the baby, measured her, and did all the routine things nurses do with newborns. I was finally allowed to get out of bed and stand up, but that was short-lived when she made me try to go pee. Long story short, it did not happen. I was stuck with the I.V.'s until I finally went. The nurse brought a wheelchair and wheeled Parker and me down the hall to our room while poor Nolan was stuck walking behind in the dim, quiet hallways of the hospital in the middle of the night carrying all our stuff. We settled in as much as one can at three in the morning, and then we all fell asleep after such a productive day. Five o'clock rolled around, and it was time — I HAD TO PEE! Little did I know that the nurse hung my I.V. bags to the wall and took away the rolling cart. I couldn't find my call button fast enough! The nurse came into the room to unhook me. I made it to the toilet with such relief and started to pee. Then came my second moment of "no one told me about this part." OH THE PAIN, OH THE PAIN, OH THE PAIN! The nurse came running back into the bathroom when she heard me crying in pain. "I told you to wait so I could get the bottle to take away the pain," she said. Funny, telling a woman who just had a baby to hold her pee. After that fun instance, it was back to trying to feed Parker. The new nurse attempted to help me again, but shortly after she left, I just had the same feeling of being useless. It was not working, but the nurse seemed to think it was. But what was I to know? I was 5 hours into this new role.

A couple of diaper changes, a few hours, several quick power naps, and a nurse change later, I thought this would be it. It was a fresh day, a fresh perspective, and I was thinking to myself, *this nurse will be the one to help me get a hold of this newfound pain and confusion.* That day came and went with lots of visits and "help" from the nurse. Needless to say, I wasn't her biggest fan, and I don't think she liked me either. Then we had another nurse change, as well as a rude awakening at one in the morning to have Parker's 24-hour weight check. She was down a pound, but to them, this was "normal." As I sat there wondering if I was even feeding her anything (the baby's mouth isn't see-through, but gee, wouldn't that make life simple?), I could hear my birth class instructor in the back of my mind saying, "It's normal for babies to lose some weight after birth." I relaxed a little at that moment and fell back asleep.

Parker started shifting awake a few hours later, so I called the nurse, and to my surprise, there had been another nursing change... my best friend was back! She checked the feeding chart that we were supposed to be filling out, and all she had to say was, "You're not feeding her long enough." Ummm...how was that supposed to make me feel? It definitely did not make me feel better. After she left, I was able to finally have my first shower and put myself back to my semi-new normal. We attended our mandatory discharge class and went back to our room to pack up. We got our papers, and Nolan went home to get the car (yes, we live that close to the hospital that he could walk to get the car — so close that we walked to the hospital to be induced).

The doctor came into our room to tell me Parker's blood results were a little too low for their liking, but she could go home, and we would have to come back tomorrow for an appointment to check her levels again. I was all alone, thinking that we were in the clear, she was fine, and I must have been doing something right, but then it all came crashing down. I sat in that hospital room all alone, trying to keep it together, wondering what the problem could be. As I sat on the bed waiting for Nolan's text that he was downstairs, the doctor returned. Apologizing profusely, she told me she had made a mistake. She had read the wrong baby's chart. At that moment, I was nothing but grateful that Parker was okay, but my heart still ached for those new parents that were about to get the opposite news that their baby had to go back to the hospital for more tests. My favourite nurse in the whole entire world (sense the sarcasm) came back into the room, and she even apologized. Maybe she was human after all.

I asked her where we had to get our car seat checked and experienced yet another shocking moment. She told me that they do not do that at the hospital. "Okay, so I can just carry her out?" I asked. She said, "Yes, I just need to cut her bracelets off." And just like that, we were officially discharged. Nolan's text came quickly after, and I picked up the pillow and name board we had forgotten to pack and my brand-new baby girl wrapped in a blanket with her little itty bitty newborn hat on, no car seat, no nothing. Just me, a pillow, a name board, and this baby walking down the hallway. We walked past the nurse's station, out the doors, into the elevators, through the lobby, and out the main doors. Nolan was there waiting, and I could not get Parker buckled in fast enough to tell Nolan everything that had just happened to me in the last ten minutes he was gone. He was as relieved as I was. We got in the car, two nervous parents leaving the hospital: one nervous new father (who is usually a speed demon) and a nervous new mom (who is a back seat driver, literally, in this case). As I sat beside Parker for our quick trip in the car, getting mad at every pothole Nolan decided to hit, I was in shock and awe that this baby was now OUR responsibility. Who were we to raise a kid? How are we supposed to know what to do when she cries? The questions came flooding in. WTF are we doing?!?! Parker was very, very unplanned. After already feeling like I failed this helpless baby, I questioned if we made the right decision. I knew I loved Nolan, but we were not even a full year into our relationship. Sure, we lived together and were planning to maybe one day have kids and get married, but who were we at this moment to bring another human into this world?

We were home, the three of us. Our new normal. The world seemed like it had just been turned upside down. Then the time came...it was inevitable that Parker needed to eat. So I grabbed my breastfeeding pillow, sat down in her nursery, and got ready. Nolan brought Parker to me, and it just wasn't working. I had learned how to hand express and feed the baby from a cup in our birthing class. *Great, I thought, I will try this.* We found a medicine cup in the cupboard and thought it would be perfect. The thought of calling my doctor or anyone for help did not even cross my mind — we had a doctor's appointment the next day. How hard could the next twenty-four hours be? The hand expression worked, the cup feeding worked, and it was all going to "plan." The doctor's appointment was upon us. They weighed her. She was down again, too much for their liking. She recommended I go see a lactation consultant; I was not against it but needed to figure out what to do in the meantime. My doctor's secretary mentioned a sample of formula, but my doctor knew I wanted to try everything first before formula became my number one option. We left the doctor's office with an appointment booked for a week later to check Parker's weight again but still left wondering what to do. When we arrived home, I called the lactation consultant, and low and behold, I could not get an appointment until the following week. Another loss. I am usually pretty lucky, but it just felt like everything was against me that week. That night led to more hand expression just trying to get enough, but it wasn't. The next morning came with great frustration and a trip to our local baby store. Seven hundred dollars later, I had a breast pump. I thought *I am going to need the best, so this baby can have "the best."* I wish I could go back to that moment and make something go awry just so I could have saved my money. I truly believe everything happens for a reason, but that stupid pump is still sitting in the top of Parker's closet collecting dust today.

I followed every instruction to a T in that pump manual — sanitized it all properly, dried it all properly, and did everything else I was supposed to do. I even downloaded the app so I could track how much I pumped. And so it began. I sat down, and everything was going fine. I had read online to start low and go until you feel pain, and then go back down one level. Okay, fine. Well, you see, I have a high pain tolerance (clearly why I didn't even know I was in labour), so I get to the top level and feel no pain. I just left the pump on the highest level, and the heavenly white liquid just started to flow into the bottle. One bottle was a little more full than the other, but I did not even think twice about it. I input it all into my app and poured all the milk into storage bags. If it worked this well this time, then this must be how it happens every time, right? The week continued and things went well. I was comfortable with exclusively pumping. I had accepted that this was going to be our new normal.

The appointment for the lactation consultant was still on our calendar, and the thought crossed my mind to cancel and give it to a mom who really needs help. But I kept it anyway. When we arrived, we were given a quick little tour and then got down business. Here I was, sitting in a tiny room with two strangers, breasts out like it was my day job. My mom was not kidding when she said you check your dignity at the door when you have a baby. They set me up with the same breast pillow I had at home, and I thought it was great that now I would know the exact setup I should have when I got home. We tried several different positions, but Parker just did not want to latch. They checked her mouth to make sure she was not tongue-tied — all good there. Then the wonderful nurse decided we should try a nipple shield. Well, OMG, it worked. I wish I had known about this before I even had Parker. WHAT A LIFE CHANGER! Parker was crying like I had never heard her cry before, only for the simple fact that I think she knew what was coming. Pure joy: Parker was eating, and it did not hurt like I had been warned about. I had switched my mindset from exclusively pumping to *I got this!*

And then we went home. The first few feedings went well...then it was just downhill from there, and back to pumping I went. I had accepted it, as that was already my plan. Several weeks later, that also started going downhill. I thought it was the pump. I contacted the company, and they sent a new one right away. I set it all up just like the last one but got nothing. Just nothing. I was so upset. I had just spent all this money and was getting nothing. NOTHING. I was upset, frustrated, mad, you name it. Thanks to Google, I chalked it up to a blocked duct or mastitis, which were both treatable. I could get through this. I called my doctor and set up an appointment. Between that phone call and my appointment, I tried all the tricks I could find on the internet: tea, lactation cookies, beer, wine, planking while pumping, hot showers...the list went on and on. Nothing helped. I explained everything to my doctor, and she said it was like my body had made up its mind that it was done with breastfeeding. While doing all my research, I found out there was a pill that was supposed to help women lactate. I asked my doctor, and she said the side effects were not ideal and since my body had just "stopped," it would be best for Parker to go onto formula. We had already given her a bottle here and there while my supply was dwindling away, so I knew she could handle it. That night we officially made the switch to 100% formula, and at the end of the day, I would not change it for the world.

All I could think of during this whole time was *WTF, why me?* I am a huge planner and love to know everything ten steps before it even happens. This little bundle of joy of mine really threw a wrench into this plan of my life. At the end of the day, my baby was fed, she was happy, she was growing, and I was even happier for it. If I can leave you with one piece of advice, it would be to not listen to the "norm" of life. Do what makes you happy. Screw everyone else and their negative judgmental thoughts!

CHAPTER 7

Kaitlin Wilson

PHOTO: **BRIAN WILSON**

@KAITJWJLSON

am a Mom to two beautiful children who are 6 and 2. My son is smart, sensitive, and so creative. My daughter is fiery, clever, and so funny. I live a simple life with my husband's amazing musical skills and my love for the outdoors and reading. In my husband's wedding vows, he called us "hobbits," and I remember a family member asking me what this meant. To us, it means enjoying quality food, comfy furnishings, and making a quiet home full of love and learning. We have a small extended family and a group of wonderful friends who are like family. My husband and I met in high school, we went to University together, and we established our careers before we decided we wanted to start a family. We grew up together and went through bumps along the way to finding our perfect careers and building a life together. Both of us are planners, and we do not make rash decisions; although now, as a 40-year-old parent to young children, I understand the value of having children younger when you have more energy. I know that our paths led us to this time and I focus my life around the belief that things happen for a reason.

We are connected to our community through supporting businesses and living close to our jobs. I had always wanted to be a mother. I went in fully knowing that it would not be all roses and cuddles. It truly has not been easy (from many sleepless nights to worrying all the time, all-day morning sickness...you know the drill), but I feel like I rock it pretty hard. I went through postpartum like so many mothers, but having my support network was key. I realized early on how important sleep was for my mental health. I knew after a stint of sleepless nights I needed to rest when I could. The amazing Mommy groups and my own wonderful mother and mother-in-law were key players as I navigated the early days. I know the online and community groups are not for everyone, but I met the most amazing women (and some rock star Dads) with whom I could laugh and cry along the way.

Like many people who have aging parents, we are in a time where we are pulled in many directions that no one can prepare us for. Many times I have fallen into bed and wondered how I could possibly balance anything else. This past year tested all of my everything. Yes, there was a pandemic, but it was bigger for us. In January 2020 we were railroaded with the news that my beautiful, amazing mom had Stage 4 endometrial cancer. I had been through news like this before when my father got his news 7 years ago — Stage 4 brain cancer. Navigating hospitals and doctors is not something new for me. My brother and I tried so hard to bring love and light to her with optimism and positivity, but we both completely fell apart. Then restrictions started happening. We could not join her for appointments. She was having issues making sure she was asking all the questions. Dropping her off for chemo was devastating, but we were amazed by her strength through it all. We had moments of success — we had photos from her last day of chemo and information from her doctors that made us excited for more years together. She was truly our all-star. I also had times where I had to take a little break and just be away from it all. I am sure so many of you can relate to this feeling when someone you love is fighting for their life.

Fast forward to October. I had gone back to work after some fun in the summer together with special Sunday night dinners and sweet visits with her. Mom was showing signs of pain similar to her original diagnosis. We all tried again to build our strength. I took some days off. I went over as much as I could to be with her. Visits were restricted in the hospital. I put on this brave face that I had to dig very deep to find. Coming home to my own children was filled with snuggles and the deepest conflicting pain that I could not always be by her side. I kept thinking *we have to get her out of there*. I thought we had time. She made the choice to come home from the hospital. It was a hard choice, but making her comfortable was important.

I started to see the signs that she did not have much longer. I saw them with my aunt and with my dad. The sparkle that is in the eyes of someone full of life was not there. The pain and the pain medication were taking that away. We set up care for her and again tried our best to stay positive. I was so thankful that my brother could take time to be with her, but I also saw the strain and the need for a break for him. Something told me that her sister and brother needed to make their way to us. I wanted to make it at work until Halloween and then planned to take November off to be with her. We planned for my kids' favourite holiday and then got the news she had passed. My whole world fell apart. It was 6:45 am on October 31st. It was pitch black out, and I was crying on the front step. My beautiful children had no idea why I was crying and tried to help me with hugs.

The moments from there on are hard to recall. I remember calling my brother, hugging my aunt and uncle, clinging to whatever I could. Their hugs felt so good after being in quarantine for so long. I remember the sun was coming up, and it was so wonderful that day, but all I wanted to do was crawl into bed in the dark. I remember turning the corner to see an ambulance and police cars. I remember the kindness of everyone around me. The sweet words from the paramedic. The wonderful nurse who came to help.

To make matters worse, my husband broke his ankle. He needed me too. Getting back home, I talked to myself the whole way. My kids were so excited about Halloween. I was not ready to tell them. I like to research everything before I dive into something challenging. I knew I needed to consult experts before explaining that our beautiful Gran was no longer here.

I called my best friend and she said all the right things. She dropped everything and came to my rescue. I remember thinking, *how in the hell do I go on from this?* How does a person honour their grief and still give something to their children? I think my kids sensed my pain. Somehow, with the support of family and friends, I was able to take my kids to a few houses to trick or treat. My son said, "it was the best Halloween ever." Somehow I found that strength inside of me. It came from the love that my mother showed me. I missed her with all my heart, but I still felt her love and support all around me.

We decided to hold off on a celebration of life until we could all be together and restrictions were lifted. The love shown to us from family and friends still takes my breath away. Our fridge was full of food, and we had so many memories shared with us. Social media may have its issues, but it did help bring us together when we physically could not be together.

So that is my story. It was hard to write, but also so good to share.

I thought long and hard about how to proceed with this chapter. A good friend told me she admired my strength. I was surprised by this, and then I did some self-reflection. What I can offer are some tips or help to navigate grief and to be a parent. It's not easy, and it's messy and frustrating, just like many other aspects of parenting. I've had many WTF moments, but I continue to grow. Here is what I have learned.

Being Pulled In All Directions

As an adult, many of us feel a pull in a variety of directions. Balancing work, partnerships, friendships, parent responsibilities, extended family support, taking care of yourself...the list goes on. When someone is sick in your life and needs help, many things have to go on the back burner. For me, I had such amazing support at work, so it was not as big of an issue. However, I had the most difficulty being away from my children. They had an amazing time with their dad, but I often came home emotionally drained, and they picked up on this. Their behaviour would shift, and I would become frustrated. The results were yelling, threats, and lots of tears. This is not my parenting style. I remember thinking, *WHY CAN'T ONE THING IN MY LIFE BE EASY?* There was no breakthrough moment, but I did find that if I could get home before they were home, wash my face, take a breath, use all my relaxing lavender oils, and meet them with calmness, then our time together would not be as frustrating. Honouring my own emotions and finding some sliver of peace helped me to not match their complex emotions with my own. My mom was the one I would complain to about the hardships of parenting. I couldn't bring this negativity into her world either. She was fighting for her life. Talking to my partner about what I needed was key. I was already holding together so much that I needed to trust and lean on him. He was always asking what I needed. I am forever thankful for that!

Advocate

Time and energy are precious. Doctors and nurses are amazing superheroes, but their time and energy are often spread so thin. When my dad was sick, I remember leaving thinking, *I should have asked about* _____. I didn't want to bug or seem demanding of anyone. I learned that when faced with big decisions and the need for medical support or intervention, we all need to advocate. This is especially important if your loved one is elderly and in total shock. I allowed myself the time to be emotional, but then I dug deep into some part of me and sort of detached. I became, in a way, dispassionate. I let go of my emotional connection and passionate side. I was polite with our team of doctors and nurses, and I learned to ask about things. If I had more questions, I followed up. It was helpful because it almost felt like this was happening to someone else. Now, a therapist probably would not recommend this, and I had to do some serious work emotionally after, but I often felt like I had covered all the bases: ask all the important questions, write things down so you can remember, and have all the information you need. We've all done internet searches when we are not sure about something. Researching is important, but making sure your medical team is covering all the bases is the most important.

Honouring Your Grief

After the shock of my mom's death had started to sink in, all I wanted to do was lie in bed and be in the dark alone. When you have little people who need you, this is not possible. Maybe you can sneak in a nap here and there or maybe let them watch an extra show or movie, but these little people need you every second of every day. At least mine do. I found myself sneaking off to the bathroom to cry or take some deep breaths. I would take the dog for an extra-long walk and would catch myself holding my breath so I would not break down on the busy street. When my dad passed, a friend told me you can have those hard days. **You will have those hard days.**

Embrace them and honour your grief. Sit in your grief and let it flow. But the next day or the day after that, dust yourself off, and do what you need to be somewhat normal again. Drink all the water, watch that silly comedian, give all the hugs, and share when you are ready. The grief will never go away, but it does get slightly less painful. On my better days, we would head outside for brief stints of time, and I would feel good. I realized I needed some time off work. I would head over to my mom's house to just sit and look at things...to hold onto things that she had loved and held on to. This time was so valuable. I felt so tired all the time as well. She would often write down words of wisdom on little sheets of paper. I cherish those now. It takes so much energy when you're so upset that you need to rest when you can.

When I was ready, one thing I did was reach out on social media. It might not be for everyone to share so openly, but I decided to take seven days and share pictures and stories of my beautiful mother. They were stories about her life, who she was, and how important she was to everyone. Some were funny stories (e.g., dressing me like a California Raisin on Halloween — I looked more like a furry purple monster), and some were about her being a pack rat (e.g., finding a hair perming kit from the late 80s). I talked about her childhood, my dad, our childhood, and her work. A friend had done this about her mother, and I remember saying how wonderful it was to learn more about her mom. I shared a speech one of her students made when he graduated grade eight. These artifacts were so wonderful and healing. Without the finality of a funeral, many of us were looking for connection and closure. The response was amazing, and people I hadn't heard from in many years commented about how much they enjoyed my posts. This made my heart sing. It was one small step in healing my broken heart.

My therapist had shared about visualizing those around me like they are countries on a map (I love a good visualization, and my background is in Geography, so he had me hooked right away!).

Some people on my map are closer to me (e.g., my husband, my kids, my brother), and they hold more space. Other people may move closer or further away depending on relationships and connections. They are all a part of your world and have an impact on you — some more than others. He said when a person passes away, their country may darken slightly and grow a bit smaller or further away, but their spot is always there. They have impacted your life and remain a huge part of who you are. I ended up drawing my map, and it was beautiful. It made me feel so good to see all the connections, and then to think about all the maps that I was a part of and that my Mom was a part of. I appreciated this activity, and although it was very tough, it was another important part of my healing journey.

Explaining Death To Your Child

This last part of my chapter was tough to write. My son is very perceptive and empathetic. He is also emotional like me. He sees and hears everything, even if you think he isn't paying attention. His memory is amazing. After my Mom passed, I was not prepared to explain it to him right away. I felt I needed to be in a better place, and I am always the researcher, so I wanted to make sure I approached it the best way I could. From all the things I read one important point stood out to me: be honest and explain the reality of death. My husband and I agreed that we needed to keep it simple for him. We discussed our plan, and we picked a day when it was just us together. I ordered the most amazing book about a fox who passes and how all the animals are sad about him not being around the forest. They all share stories about the fox. A tree starts to grow where he was, and the animals all enjoy the tree. We read the story together and explained how his wonderful Gran had passed. Our amazing boy said, "I already knew that." He expressed how he had wondered where Gran was and how sad I was. He asked many questions that we answered the best we could. He wanted to see her house and confirm things for himself. Afterwards, we treated ourselves to some fast food and played some games. I was so proud and sad all at once. My daughter is still too young to understand it all, but her amazing brother will help her as she grows.

Sometimes we get it right as a parent. Maybe I raise my voice a bit too much, maybe my house is not perfectly clean all the time, maybe I am not always the gentle parent I want to be, but sometimes things work the way we were hoping they would. My mom taught me that being present in your child's life and honouring their emotions is more important than sparkling countertops or name brand clothing (my kids' clothes are mostly hand-me-downs and my countertops are far from perfect). Mom loved watching me shrug my shoulders as my son covered himself in mud. She cherished hugs. She adored buying things for my daughter especially. She giggled as I tried to get my son's socks on just perfect (something I always needed as a kid). She reminded me to nap now and then and how much better I would feel after. She will always be with me — a huge part of my map, with her light shining so bright on us all. Dear reader, if you have lost someone so important, my love and light shine to you. Continue to shine, you beautiful soul.

CHAPTER 8

KAYLA MUNRO

PHOTO: **MONIKA PARR PHOTOGRAPHY**
@INSPIRINGYOURS
INSPIREYOURNICUJOURNEY.CA

I always knew I wanted to be a mom. That, and a teacher. Both roles have always just *'fit'* me. I'm organized by nature, even though my mom would tell you I'm also messy. I love learning and teaching. And I have always loved being around children. I've been told that my life has kind of just *"fallen into place."* I graduated from my dream teaching program at 23, married my high school love at 25, and had a baby at 26. Sounds pretty good, right? Then I was hit with what I now know was just a bump, but at the time felt like an impossible mountain.

I thought motherhood would be easy. I thought it would be a natural transition for me, being a daycare kid turned teacher who had been around kids and babies my entire life. HA HA. Now, as I'm typing that out, even I think I sound ridiculous. I don't think there is any way motherhood could be considered *"easy,"* but I thought I would fall right into my new role. And then, somehow, I suddenly ended up in premature labour and having a baby at only 33 weeks. The NICU became my new home, and I had NO CLUE what the f*ck I was doing.

My name is Kayla. I'm a mother, teacher, and self-proclaimed *"inspirer."* I know it doesn't sound like a real word, but I promise it is. I've always been the one to find some light in dark situations, but the story of my son is different. It's not one I found light in right away, but I know now that this is part of me and my story.

Let's rewind a bit, because I said motherhood would be easy, right? Well, I had no reason to think anything would go wrong with our baby. It didn't take us too long to get pregnant, my pregnancy was low-risk, and I was able to have my care with midwives. Everything was going great. There was no reason to think I wouldn't make it to full-term — no reason to think our baby would end up in the NICU. And yet, that's where I was. On Halloween night in 2020, a few hours after some *adult* fun (sorry, family members who are reading this), I started bleeding. Now, I had heard that this was super common this far along (I was 32 weeks, 4 days at this point), so I figured it would go away on its own.

Then, at 2 am, I woke up to some cramping and what I thought was a lot of blood. I called our midwives, and they were amazing. They went through all of my bloodwork, ultrasounds, asked tons of questions, and made me feel a lot better. They said it was normal, but I could go in to get checked if I wanted to. I decided not to because it was Halloween night, and I knew the hospitals would be crazy. I would know if I was in labour, right? Apparently not.

To make a long story short, the bleeding stopped but I had on and off cramping throughout the next day. There was no bleeding, though, so I figured I had just pushed myself too hard, and needed to slow down. I was still cramping on and off the next day and night, but nothing terrible. If I'm being honest – apologies for the TMI – I thought I had constipation cramps. They were actually, I would later find out, early labour contractions. Who knew? I sure didn't.

The next day was a Monday, and as I got ready for school, I complained to my husband that I was so tired and achy. I am a teacher and was in a long-term position at the time. I got ready and taught all morning, but my teaching partner in the room could tell I was off and was helping out wherever she could. I remember standing up before lunch and feeling this immense pressure. And then when I went to the bathroom, there was blood again.

So there I was, in our school supply room, calling my midwives. After letting my Vice Principal know that I needed to leave, I was on my way home to get my husband – and having some pretty intense cramps. On the drive to the hospital, I had this feeling to time the cramping I was having (now I know they were contractions, but I had NO IDEA then).

Just to give you the full idea of how clueless I was, I called my mom and told her that I was fine; I just needed to be checked, and then we would be on our way home. Maybe I'd be on bed rest or something. Gosh, thinking back now, I literally had no f*cking idea what I was doing. HOW did I not know I was in labour? I guess it happens more often than you'd think. When we got to the hospital, my contractions (keep in mind, I was still telling the midwives that they were "cramps" at this point) were 2 minutes apart. After being monitored for about 25 minutes, the "cramps" were getting worse, and the midwives realised I was likely in labour.

When the OB came to check me, his exact words were, "Well, you are 6-7 cm dilated. You are having this baby now!" I didn't even have time to panic because the contractions were that intense. About 30 minutes and one failed epidural later, at 3:14pm, we had a 4lb 5oz baby boy – Cohen James.

Now let me tell you...to say that I was in SHOCK is an understatement. I don't think everything hit me until about 2am, as I was sitting beside my baby, who was intubated (if you've seen someone intubated before, you know how scary it is), with wires and monitors everywhere. It didn't feel real. This wasn't supposed to happen. I was supposed to have a calm, uncomplicated birth. The 8lb squishy baby. And then go home for our family to meet him. What was I supposed to do now?

I was discharged 24 hours after giving birth, and we had to leave without our son. I had no idea what I was going to do. How was I supposed to be a mom without having my baby with me? This was not what I had imagined. It wasn't even something I had thought was a possibility.

Our NICU journey was a fairly "easy" one, although I don't think you can call the NICU easy. I went from having no idea that you could get a burn from an IV to seeing my tiny baby's IV need to be moved because of one. I went from having no clue what an *adjusted age* meant to using the term every day. Cohen's main issue in the NICU was his breathing. Usually, when you are in early labour, the doctors will try to stop or slow it so that they can give you steroid shots for the baby's lungs. Unfortunately, I wasn't able to get them because my labour went so quickly. When Cohen was first born, he cried very quickly, which the doctors were very happy about. They even let me see him before taking him to the NICU because of this. But then he started to decline. He had to be intubated and given a drug to help his immature lungs. This was probably the scariest part looking back, but I was still in so much shock that I didn't know what to think at the time. Thankfully, he was only intubated for a few hours and then was on CPAP for a day. I learned so much about premature babies during Cohen's NICU stay. It was overwhelming. This wasn't what I thought my journey would be like when becoming a mom. I thought I would know what I was supposed to do. And yet, here I was, in tears every night I had to leave our baby in the hospital.

Cohen spent 18 days in the NICU — the longest, most emotional, and most helpless days I've ever had. I shared a lot of our story on my Instagram page as we were going through it. I smiled at the camera most days and gave updates on how he was doing. I had no idea if I was being a good mom while he was in the NICU. Should I be staying with him overnight? Was I hands-on enough with the nurses? Was I getting in their way too much? Was it okay that I was sharing so much? Should I be crying this much? I had absolutely no clue what the f*ck I was doing.

But guess what? I didn't need to know what I was doing. **You don't need to know what you're doing as a mom because our babies are all different. That's the way it's supposed to be.** And the NICU is a place where every baby, and every mom, needs something different. I had no idea how to change the diaper of a 4lb preemie, but the amazing nurses taught me how. And when it was time to breastfeed that tiny baby, I had help. It was okay that I didn't know what I was doing. Actually – it was expected.

I didn't know that then, but I know it now. And I know it for you. You do NOT need to know what you are doing all the time. No matter if it's when you're having a baby, starting a new business, or even just beginning a new hobby. **Unless you have studied the subject your entire life and have some sort of degree or diploma in the topic, I don't think anyone expects you to know what you're doing. We put that expectation on ourselves.**

Now, as if going into spontaneous preterm labour and having a preemie wasn't enough, the universe was like, "HERE! Now navigate bringing that little baby home in the middle of a freaking PANDEMIC." Um, WHAT?

I mean, realistically, no one knew what to do when this pandemic hit. And I really hope no one expected new (especially first-time) moms to know how to handle bringing home a baby in the middle of it all.

When we found out we were pregnant with Cohen, we had just gone into lockdown, and Ontario's March break for schools had been extended. I'm not a permanent teacher yet — I was only in a long-term position, so it was very nerve-wracking to think that I could be let go if we didn't go back to school. At the time, my husband also worked on construction sites, so the possibility of him being let go for a bit was another scary thought. Being pregnant in a pandemic wasn't fun, but I felt like I was able to protect my son because he was still inside me. I knew that I didn't need to go out often — I could distance myself from everyone, and it just seemed easier. But sitting in the NICU, thinking about how I now had to bring this tiny baby home and protect him from not only the normal things a new mom worries about, but also from COVID-19? I had no clue what I should do. Cohen was also born during RSV[2] season — something I didn't know about before having a preemie, but yet another thing to worry about.

Telling your family that they not only had to be pretty much *scheduled* to meet your newborn, but they also had to wear masks and hold him in a blanket was not fun. It was such a weird feeling. All I wanted to be was happy, watching our families meet our son for the first time, but I was also terrified. I was so scared that he would get sick. I was so scared we would end up back in the hospital. Kangaroo care (also known as skin to skin) was pretty much all we did while Cohen was in the NICU, except while he was under the bilirubin lights. I had a ton of time to scroll my phone and worry about him. I found all the NICU moms I could on Instagram and

---

[2] Respiratory Syncytial Virus

followed all the accounts that had anything to do with the NICU. Something I noticed in these NICU stories that I wouldn't say was common but did happen a few times was that babies that leave the NICU sometimes end up back there a few days later. I was so scared I wouldn't know what to do when we got home. I mean, he was hooked up to vital monitors until the night before we took him home. If his heart rate dropped or he wasn't breathing great, I could tell just by looking at the monitor. How was I supposed to know without the monitors there?

I know postpartum anxiety is fairly common now, but I didn't realize how much it affected me until I looked back on it. For weeks I wouldn't sleep properly because I would wake up so often just to make sure Cohen was breathing. This was not what I imagined motherhood to be. I imagined being tired, but never terrified. That's something that's not talked about as much when you get pregnant — that not only will you love this little human with all that you have, but you will also be downright terrified something will happen to them.

The first few months of Cohen's life, we were in lockdown. It wasn't a full-on "stay at home" order, but still a lockdown. We had to make decisions on when our family was able to see Cohen. Honestly, I looked to our doctors a lot for answers. I had no idea what I should be doing. There's no manual on raising a baby during a pandemic that tells you how to do everything right. Would our families be mad that they didn't get to see him often? Would they be mad that they had to wear masks? Would they be offended when I made sure they washed their hands before touching him? I felt that no matter what we chose for our son, we would be judged for not doing the 'right" thing. I guess that's how it can be with motherhood, though. No matter what decisions you make, there will always be someone to say you did it wrong. This doesn't help when you already feel like you have no clue if you're doing anything right.

These first few months were hard because I always felt like I wasn't doing enough. I wasn't cleaning the house enough. I wasn't paying enough attention to my husband. I wasn't talking with my friends often. I'm sure the fourth trimester feels like that for a lot of women, but I think if I hadn't been honest in my feelings, it would have consumed me. I had to tell my husband when I needed a break. I used Instagram to show the easy and the hard parts I was going through, and it gave me a bit of an outlet. Looking back, I probably should have started therapy. It definitely would've helped. And as I'm writing this, I still haven't reached out yet. I've looked into the benefits we get through my husband's work, and I've searched for therapists in our area. I even found a group of therapists I think I'll like, but I haven't sent that first email yet. Why? Because I have no idea what I'm doing. I have no idea what to expect. I like understanding how things work, and I need to know what I'm walking into. With this, I have no idea what therapy will bring up. I am terrified to start, and honestly that's probably the very reason I need to. I know I'll get there, and my hope is that by the time you are reading this, I'll have at least started. But for now, I know that I am doing my best. I'm taking time for myself, and I'm learning how to balance being a mom and being me. But the trauma of the NICU will always be there. It's part of who I am now, and I needed to find a way to both honour that and help other families who are going through what we did.

Not too long after Cohen was born, I came up with an idea for a non-profit/charity. I wanted to be able to give back to the NICU Cohen was born in by supporting the families that were going through it. As I researched support for not only me but my husband, I noticed a lack of support for partners and families of NICU babies. When a baby is born premature or has to spend time in the NICU, it's not only the baby and mom who are affected. The partner, grandparents, siblings, aunts, uncles, and so many more also feel the effects of that little baby being in the NICU. Sure, they may not be living it directly, but I know that both my mother and mother-in-law were distraught to see my husband and me going through our NICU stay with Cohen. Thankfully, we had a very supportive circle around us, and we still do. But not everyone with a NICU baby does. And so, I wanted to do something that would give strength, love, and support to all the NICU families — past, present, and future families of preemie and NICU babies. So where do I even start? I had absolutely no clue. So I just – started. We started with a name. Inspire Your NICU Journey. Right now, we are focusing on raising money for our "Trees of Strength" program. Essentially, we're raising money for gift card trees for NICU families at Markham Stouffville Hospital because the amount of money spent on food, gas, and parking while having a baby in the NICU is ridiculous. If we can help with that just a bit, it would be amazing. After launching our first donation campaign for the month of June, we have gotten $700 of the $750 goal we set out to reach. In just a WEEK. I was in tears. The fact that people wanted to support my idea to help others has been overwhelming.

Now I have no idea what I want this to become, and let me be clear — I have NO CLUE WTF I AM DOING — not just in this, but with motherhood and life in general. But I'm trying, and dreaming, and just plain doing. And that's what matters. Sometimes, you just have to start and learn along the way.

I never thought I would be sitting here, writing a chapter for a book, holding my baby that was born at just 33 weeks, and building a charity inspired by him. But I think that's what is so amazing about life. **You never know what the f*ck you are doing. And that's okay. You're not supposed to.**

CHAPTER 9

KRYSTAL HAYDEN

PHOTO: **GYPSI SPIRIT PHOTOGRAPHY BY TRACY**
@KRYSTAL_0X0
KRYSTALHAYDEN.COM

I was one of those little girls who played with baby dolls and was obsessed with babies. I started babysitting at 11 years old for multiple families and always enjoyed being with children. In high school, I even loved the parenting class. Basically, I could not wait to have babies of my own one day.

When I had this image in my head of motherhood, I pictured sweet, loving, happy babies who grew up to be those same adorable children with a mother who was always happy and loving motherhood. Well let me tell you...that is NOT what I got.

My oldest, Kristopher, was a great baby who slept amazingly, ate everything he was given, was polite, independent, and oh so smart.

Basically, he was the baby and toddler that tricks you into wanting all the babies.

Then, along came our daughter, Lexi. She would not get out of the womb, would not sleep alone, would not go to bed until midnight most nights, always wanted to be with someone else, and oh my gosh, was so freaking sassy – basically the opposite of what her brother had been.

My husband was content with just the two children. We had our boy and girl. Therefore we had the perfect family, right? I always felt like there was a piece missing, though. That missing piece arrived in April 2016 – a month before his due date. And let me tell you... since he showed up, Bennett has kept us on our toes with his wild ways. He is the comic relief we never knew we needed in our family; he was our final puzzle piece and completed our family.

As happy as I was with our new family of five, that final pregnancy was when everything changed for me. I had not experienced Postpartum Depression in the past, and I was going through a lot of changes with Kristopher at the same time with his own mental health. I did not understand what was going on with him or how to help him, and it made me feel like my world was crumbling around me. Not only was I navigating all of these challenges, but I was also doing it alone. For anyone who knows me, they know I do NOT like asking for help, so this was a very dark time for me. Looking back now, I know that I am not the only one who has gone through times like this. I know I am not the only mom that has felt embarrassed, ashamed, or like a terrible mother because life just gets far too overwhelming, and you feel like you cannot get back on track. I know that by talking about it, I could very well help another momma out there who is also struggling just like I was. So as uncomfortable as this may make me, I hope this helps at least one other mom out there see that there is light at the end of the tunnel, and you are not alone. **You are never alone!**

My name is Krystal. I am a wife to Corey, mother to Kristopher, Lexi, and Bennett and two pups Molly and Hershey, and an entrepreneur. Corey works away from home anywhere from a week to eight weeks at a time and could be a few hours away to provinces away, so it isn't always easy for him to get home quickly. I run a skincare business solely online, helping team members do the same, and I have an Etsy business that I run out of my home office. I also homeschooled my two oldest from September 2017 until April of this year when they decided they wanted to go back to school. So, you could say I kind of "do it all!"

As I mentioned, everything started to change when I was pregnant with Bennett. At that point in my life, I was right in the thick of feeling like I was failing my other two children. I couldn't figure out what I needed to do to get Kristopher the help he needed for his own mental health. This was extremely challenging and frustrating. This would be the first time as a mother that I saw first-hand that sometimes you have to really stand your ground and fight when you know your intuition is telling you something and doctors aren't listening. Working through this with Kristopher was in itself an extremely stressful and long journey. It took us years to get any answers. Now, even though it is Kristopher's mental health journey, I mention it because I am pretty sure that going through all of that while pregnant is what finally brought my depression to the forefront. Corey was gone a lot for work, and he really had no idea what I was dealing with at home. He didn't really see a lot of what was happening in that first year or have to deal with every doctor's appointment. For a while, this was a situation that I did put on a happy face for and try to pretend that everything was alright because I thought I was doing something wrong as a mother. I didn't realize that maybe something was actually truly happening inside this poor little guy's mind that he didn't understand, nor did I. I went through doctors telling me that I was wrong about the way we went about our parenting, even though I really do not believe that a doctor or anyone has the right to say anything if they are not living in that parent's shoes. I had doctors not want to listen to me about what was going on at home because it all seemed fine when we were in the office, so I just felt like I looked like a crazy person – it really got to the point that I started to honestly question if I was just going crazy! This journey started when I was pregnant in 2015. We finally got a full diagnosis this past December 2020, which made me realize that I absolutely was not crazy...and to any other parent out there that knows deep down that something is going on with your child medically — FIGHT FOR THEM, because if you do not then no one else will! It was mentally, emotionally, and physically draining going through this journey, especially feeling so lost and alone.

Through dealing with everything with Kristopher, I still had a toddler to take care of as well. So, of course, this made me feel like a terrible mother yet again because I felt like my daughter was getting pushed to the back burner and not getting enough attention. As mothers, we can truly only stretch ourselves so thin before we burn ourselves out.

Bennett apparently couldn't wait to join in on all of our fun since he decided to come a month early. The night before I had him, I was doing a launch party for a new consultant on my Rodan + Fields team, and Corey was at a tattoo expo. After we both finished what we were doing, I said that I thought I should get checked out because I was pretty sure he was coming that weekend (I also had a table booked at a big convention that weekend, so go figure he would decide to come!). Long story short, the hospital sent me home Friday, I went to the convention Saturday (even though Laura told me heck no, I wasn't! What can I say? I'm stubborn!), but I didn't last very long before I went back to the hospital. My birth plan this time around was to hopefully have a VBAC, but once again I felt like the doctors were not listening to me. When I asked if they could give me something to move the process along since I wasn't progressing, they just brushed over it since the machines weren't showing my contractions. My contractions were all back contractions, and the machines didn't pick them up. So, I told them to just take me in for another Caesarean, and by that evening, I was holding a healthy seven-pound baby boy. So once again, my intuition was right... there's no way that at SEVEN pounds and completely healthy, he was not ready to join the world.

I was up and moving around so much faster than when I had my emergency Caesarean with Lexi – the nurses actually forgot to check on me as often as they were supposed to since I didn't need them. Now, since I felt so great and hate asking for help, I came home with the mindset that I could surely do it all myself. With Corey working on the road a majority of the time, I typically do need to do it all myself. I did end up pushing myself a bit too much and had to remind myself that I did just have major surgery, so I had to take it back a couple notches and let my body have the time to heal.

It wasn't until between four and six months postpartum that I finally came to terms with the feeling that something just didn't feel right, and I asked my doctor what was going on with me. I was ashamed, embarrassed, and felt like a terrible mother.

Why couldn't I get my mountains of dishes done?

Why do I have clothes everywhere – not knowing anymore which baskets are clean and which are dirty?

Why do I feel like just getting in my car and running away?

Why am I crying so damn much?

Why doesn't anyone see that I am drowning?

I felt judged by those closest to me, especially when my house looked like it had been hit by three hurricanes. When my doctor diagnosed me with postpartum depression around August/September

2016, he started me on antidepressants. I was breastfeeding, so they had to be safe for Bennett as well. I experienced side effects from multiple medications that I was put on, such as extreme fatigue, nausea, dizziness, and no appetite. I went through a lot of different medications and combinations until I finally found one that actually worked – which wasn't until late 2019. It is probably worth mentioning that when I finally found one that worked for me, I also started seeing a neurologist because I have suffered terrible headaches/migraines since I was twelve years old. So, she was trying to find a medication that worked for me as well as for my migraines. Once we found the correct medication combination, it was a huge change for me. I know medication doesn't work for everyone, but it did for me.

At this point, it was no longer postpartum depression and was just a diagnosis of depression and anxiety. At different points throughout the last six years, I have dealt with things in very unhealthy ways, such as drinking way too much and too often as well as eating poorly. These decisions led to me being even more cranky and irritated, having zero energy, sleeping whenever I could or not at all. Basically, I was not taking care of myself AT ALL. Drinking was probably one of the bigger issues. It was something that I would try to hide from Corey, even though I did not do a good job of that at all. He did not like when I would start drinking, so that, in turn, would cause issues in our relationship. I see that now, but at the time, I was very much clouded and not seeing straight because I was trying to deal with everything at once, and this was how I was choosing to deal with it. I know...not a healthy choice at all. Now, my kids were ALWAYS safe and taken care of and have always been my number one priority, but they have not always received me at my very best. I am just human like everyone else. I have been a mom for the past twelve years, and only in the past six or so months have I FINALLY learned that I have to take care of ME FIRST.

As if I didn't have enough on my plate with three kids, dealing with my mental health, my child's mental health, building a business, trying to keep a house together, and everything else that comes with adulthood and parenting...in 2017, when Kristopher was in grade three, we made the decision to start homeschooling. I home-schooled Kristopher for grades three to April of grade six and Lexi from Kindergarten until April of grade two. Since we were already homeschooling, our lives weren't disrupted as much as they could have been when the world was hit with the pandemic, which I was thankful for.

In December 2019, we decided that we were 10000% complete with our family, so I asked my doctor for a hysterectomy. YES! I completely know what you are thinking: "Krystal, that's a bit drastic; why not just have your husband get snipped or get your tubes tied?" Well, I always knew when the day came that I was finally done having babies that I would go for a hysterectomy. I had dealt with terrible menstrual cycles for years, so to me, this was one of the easiest decisions I ever made. January 2020, I went in for my surgery, and thank goodness I got in so soon since the Covid-19 pandemic hit two months later. To this day, I think it is probably the best decision I have EVER made for MY body.

In January 2021, I started working out for the first time ever in my life. I stuck to a program and completed ONE HUNDRED workouts! On top of working out, I started eating a lot better and making sure that I was drinking the proper amount of water. These things alone were making me feel 100% better and giving me so much more energy. My house was staying relatively tidy, which causes so much less stress when you're not looking at piles of laundry or dishes. I was having a drink here and there but very occasionally. On March 29th, 2021 I gave myself a new challenge to cut out alcohol completely — and to be quite honest, I haven't missed it at all. Every night the kids and I have been going for a bike ride or a walk, and we have all been sleeping so much better. It's amazing what some small changes in your life can do!

With all the changes I have made for myself this year, we have made some as a family as well when it comes to the children's schooling. We were looking at starting them all in the public school again in September 2021 when Bennett starts Kindergarten, but when the topic came up, the older two decided that they would really like to finish out the grades they were in at the school. As much as I think the homeschooling journey was much needed for our path in life, I think that the kids starting back to school was one of the best things that we could've done as a family.

Looking back to when I was younger, I think I was very much a "people pleaser," and even if I wasn't happy with a situation, I would just plaster a smile on my face. This is something my daughter and I do NOT share. She does not hide her emotions at all. It's something I love and dislike about her. You always know exactly what she is feeling just by looking at her. BUT I never want my children to feel like they have to be happy in every situation just because it is what "society" says they are supposed to do. Now that I am in my early thirties, I no longer care to please everyone or make sure everyone likes me. It has taken me a long time to get to where I am now, push my pride aside, and stop caring so much about people judging me. As long as my kids, Corey, and I are all happy and healthy, it does not matter what anyone else thinks of me. I think that having kids and wanting them to see the world differently has been a huge part of changing my views in the way I see it as well.

So, friend, if you are reading this and things sound familiar or are just hitting a little too close to home, please know that there IS a light at the end of the tunnel. Ask for help, ask questions, and FIGHT for what you and your family need right now. You are not alone on this journey; you are NEVER alone. Too many of us suffer in silence when we shouldn't, so speak up. You may feel very alone right now, and it may feel like you cannot get through this, but you are so strong, and you will come out even **stronger** than before. When you think no one is on your side, know that I am! ♥

CHAPTER 10

LAURA CHRISTINE CLARK

PHOTO: **VASKO OBSCURA**
@LAURACHRISTINECLARK @JUSTBOUGHTITHAIR
INFO@JUSTBOUGHTITHAIR.COM

I lost my sanity with my socks. One at a time, I barely noticed, until one day, I found they all were gone. I couldn't find them, and I couldn't focus. From 2019 until 2021 it felt like the end of the world for me. It took a lot of soul searching for me to get back to the carefree girl I was before the series of unfortunate events happened.

August 2019. I was sitting in a Starbucks eagerly awaiting my 5 o'clock meeting to show up. I was meeting with a marketing company I was going to be using to help me launch my new company, *Just Bought It Hair* — a hair extension and hair accessory e-commerce website that showed women how easy it is to match, install, and wear hair extensions. I had so many ideas, but I needed help to systematize my thoughts. The meeting went well, as expected. They were very prepared, and all of their ideas seemed very attractive and aligned with what I had envisioned. I hired them on temporarily to start, to see if we would be a good match. I would go on to hire them full-time after our successful launch four months later.

I was willing to put in my time, money, and effort to see this grow. The excitement I had for this little company was overwhelming. I started a YouTube channel, taking time to learn different editing programs, and I was getting pretty good at cutting scenes together. I had purchased a collection of various camera equipment online, and I was busting out content daily. We had a very successful launch. Sales were coming in hot, and influencers were reaching out begging us for products to review. We also had a few television shows approach us to come on air and showcase the brand. The *Just Bought It Hair* mailing list was growing substantially and quickly. I was getting phone calls about new opportunities left, right, and centre, and I needed help! I couldn't run this alone anymore as it was growing rapidly. My team and I celebrated hard that weekend right after the launch.

I had just had a baby, and my partner and I moved from a one-bedroom apartment to a two-bedroom when my son, Kenzo, was 6 months old. I was ecstatic to finally have a nursery for him. His room was exactly as I had pictured it would look when I was pregnant; Bright and airy with the sun shining in on the floor and a few plants in the corner. It was minimalist, white with hints of colours and toys strewn all over the bookshelves and floor. I would peek in when he would fall asleep and just stare at my beautiful baby boy and the room that I loved so much. It was so comforting, and I felt so happy and at peace playing with Kenzo in this room. I felt as though I had finally figured out my life, but I also had this nagging feeling in the back of my mind that something was too good to be true.

I was meeting with investors, suppliers, salons; you name it. We were going to trade shows on the weekends to get the word out there and the name, *Just Bought It Hair,* was spreading like wildfire. I remember watching the business's Instagram filled with messages and comments. The feedback I would hear from friends was so validating and addicting. I couldn't be more thrilled that I had found my passion and turned it into a career. With financial help from my partner, I was able to both watch our son at home and take on this entrepreneurial endeavour without the stress of having a full-time job. I felt so fortunate that I had the advantage of running this venture full-time. I had worked out a foolproof system: when the baby napped, I would record how-to videos, take product shots, or write copy for the website. When he would go to bed, I would edit or fulfill sales. I was busy, but it didn't feel like work.

I got up one night to fulfill an order that had come in, eagerly heading into my home office, ready to wrap up yet another purchase. I glanced over at my sleeping partner's phone, which had lit up, and a message popped up that read "I miss you too, baby."

My heart sank.

Things were going great…until they weren't. Cue 2020. If you were to jump to the end of April of this *fantastic* year, you would see me sitting alone in an Airbnb, crying, depressed, and all alone. I hadn't looked at sales for *Just Bought It Hair* in over a month.

I ignored it.

I despised it.

I couldn't even look at what I had built. It represented pain, resentment, and failure.

'What the fuck." "What the fuck." "What the fuck."

These were the most predominant thoughts that went through my head daily that April. In second place were, "What the absolute fuck?!" and "How did I get here?" I was distraught, inconsolable, and drinking too much.

For most of my life, I have made emotional decisions based on what I felt in the moment, not rationalizing or considering the conse- quences. I would fill my life with what looked like on the outside to be exciting thrills and experiences, but on the inside, I was a big ball of anxiety mixed with *Casamigos* (ok, ok, not much has changed...). On the outside, it looked like I was having fun and liv- ing my best fucking life, but on the inside I was miserable, running away from reality and trying to fill a void. This last year taught me to slow down, think ahead, and be responsible.

Do I now know what I am doing? No, but do I feel more confident in the decisions I am making? Also, no; but I am learning from my mistakes and taking it one day at a time! I will tell you the painful truth about how I realized that *I have no idea WTF I am doing,* but we will have to go back to January 2020.

I felt so accomplished. Sales were rapidly coming in. I couldn't believe I had actually started something that was successful! It was my dream to open an extension bar downtown, and with sales con- sistently coming in, I was hopeful that in a year I could reach out for the capital to make this dream a reality. I met with a financial advisor and an accountant to find out how to make this happen. For the first time in my life, I had a 1 year goal, a 3 year goal, and a 5 year goal. I know, right? What happened to Laura and who is this girl?! Then, of course, life happened, and my plan all fell apart. I knew it was all working out a little *too* flawlessly!

It all started the day I found out there was another woman. I know it's so fucking cliché, but that shit hurts and hurts deep. The feeling of being rejected by your partner right after having a baby when you are usually physically and sometimes (in my case) mentally at your worst is shattering. I suffered from really intense postpartum depression, and when you mix that with my deep-rooted abandonment issues, I was a mess. The anger that I felt was staggering, and it terrified me. I couldn't believe this was happening to me. You always hear about women being left by their partners, but you NEVER believe it will be you, especially six months after having a baby.

Then COVID entered stage left (or is it stage right?). In a weird way, it kind of felt like this was the restart that I needed. I had been so up in my feelings that this was a humbling crash back to earth — the wake-up call that I needed. I remember my therapist at the time said, "You know everybody's going through stuff right now." In a way, I felt as if my issues were not as big as they were played out in my head, and it really put things into perspective for me in the best way possible.

I was in the bedroom of our apartment, bawling my eyes out, slowly coming to the realization that I had to make a choice. My choice involved either staying and accepting verbal abuse and cheating or leaving it all behind. I won't lie; the thought of giving up everything and starting over terrified me. I was in fight or flight mode. I had no "stable" job, no child care, and I hadn't been working in years. Where would I even go? How would I support my son? Why did I have to give up this lifestyle that I had grown quite fond of now because of a decision that someone else made for me?

I decided to stay at our apartment, and I thought maybe we could make this contrived co-living situation work. I was in denial. There was name-calling and objects thrown regularly in our house, and at one point, I had cried so hard my eyes swelled shut. My mom would call me, begging me to leave, and I told her that I couldn't. There was something inside of me that wouldn't let me let this go even though I knew in my heart it was all over before it really began.

I woke up one day and I came to the realization that I had to make a drastic change and tough decisions had to be made. I had not come all of this way to be treated like a piece of garbage. So I proceeded to pack a small suitcase with as much as I could fit in it. I glanced into the little nursery that I loved curling up in so much, and all of the memories of Kenzo and I flooded into my mind. I knew that was the last time I would ever see this room. I packed up my belongings and my son into my little SUV, left my old life behind, and stayed in a friend's basement nanny suite for a week.

While I laid in this foreign bed after my son went to sleep and started looking for jobs, apartments, nannies, and daycare...holy shit, I was overwhelmed, and I started to cry. The tears streamed down my face until I couldn't possibly cry any harder. How do I start over? I had money saved, but the thought of doing this alone with an infant was frustrating and daunting. I remember thinking that I couldn't keep weeping in my poor friend's basement forever. I really just wanted to be alone, even though the thought of being alone scared the shit out of me. I was desperate, and I booked an Airbnb. *At least I could ugly cry all alone now.* I didn't realize it at the time, but this was my first step in a long, painful 8-month road to recovery. I look back and am so proud of myself for taking that first step.

We stayed in that Airbnb for two months, just my son and me. I wanted to be alone. I was depressed, angry, and very resentful. I had some good times in that house, as well as some of my darkest days. I was talking with a therapist daily, and it didn't seem to be helping. I was despondent and felt like nothing was going to make me feel better.

I threw my son's first birthday party in that house, which was a beautiful memory. I remember being very upset that I couldn't throw him a full birthday party, but I was also thankful for not having to be around anyone. I have always thrived on my own. I am very independent, and when I feel that is compromised, I tend to break down.

The party and planning process was a roller coaster of emotions, but it was my way of grieving. Due to it being the beginning of the pandemic, no one was seeing any of their friends or family, and I was in total isolation. If I could get through this, I could get through anything...I just didn't know it at the time.

After a few months of drinking too much, spiralling out of control, and some distressed phone calls, my mom decided to quit her job (bless her soul), and I moved in with her so she could help me with the baby. There were some days I could hear him crying and literally could not get out of bed. My mom would come knock on the door with a coffee, and I just could not move. I literally felt numb and didn't care about anything. I remember thinking, *this is rock bottom.* I was so depressed that I couldn't get out of bed even at 2 in the afternoon. I desperately tried to figure out how to get myself out of this and go back to being the person I was.

It was sometime around August 2020 that I remember thinking I needed to do something drastic to get myself out of this rut. I needed to do something for myself, so I donated my SUV to a family in need and bought a new car because sometimes you have to treat yourself! I fully understand now why people going through a midlife crisis buy a luxury car...except my midlife crisis started at 29.

I needed some stimulation, so I decided to take some courses in school to get my brain out of this funk and keep my mind off of things. I took a Literature and Philosophy course that I thoroughly enjoyed at a University downtown. I felt like it expanded how I thought about life and how I perceived events that were happening to and around me. I craved that feeling of submitting assignments and getting positive feedback, and having intellectual conversations with like-minded adults. After acing those courses, I knew it was time to start looking for a job. I felt confident and ready to get my life going again, but I didn't know where to start.

I met with a career counselor who helped me transition into the workforce again. I met with her once a week to figure out which jobs I should apply for, and she helped me build a resume to look for opportunities that I was interested in and would excel at.

But what about *Just Bought It Hair!?* The company that was too painful to face just months ago all of a sudden wasn't so scary anymore! I rebranded. I changed the look, the website, and the logo, and I was excited about it again. I started advertising and did a few photoshoots. I put my products on Amazon and started making sales again! I was hopeful for the future that my dream would not die by the time things opened up again.

I found a full-time job, because, you know...*bills,* but there was one last thing that I needed to do for myself — I needed my own space. I started looking for apartments in downtown Toronto. I needed something close to work but also close to my friends for support. After a month of meeting with my real estate agent and going to showings, I found the perfect two bedroom apartment for my Kenzo and I. When I signed the lease, I couldn't believe this was happening.

I picked up the keys to my empty apartment, went inside and sat on the floor, and burst into tears. This time they were happy tears. I had absolutely no furniture, but I was the happiest I had been in a year and a half.

I glanced into Kenzo's new nursery, and this time I didn't have that nagging feeling that it could all be stripped away. This was mine. I had come so far in such a short time, and even though I had no idea *WTF I was doing,* somehow it all came full circle and worked out for the best in the end. Will this be the last bit of conflict I will have to deal with in my life? Absolutely not, but like I said earlier...if I can get through a breakup, a COVID pandemic, and a newborn, I can get through anything!

CHAPTER 11

Lisa Stucke

@EXPANSIONEMPRESS

S o it began…my next life chapter. Unwritten and understood is the fact that I NEVER stopped thinking about my kids, not once. Please insert my broken heart anywhere on this ride along looking into my life.

Picture me, SINGLE for the first time in 24 years. I knew him for over half my life. My hourly mantra those days was that nagging thought…*WTF am I even doing?*

I knew the implications. I knew the perceived failure. I knew there was already a brighter horizon. I knew EVERYTHING was going to be ok.

Even still, I asked...*WTF am I even doing?* I had ZERO clue. And so it was.

On July 1st, 2012, I moved out of the home I had shared with my partner. I left and never looked back, except to acknowledge the obvious pain we inflicted on our kids by our separation.

It wasn't pretty. I was 46 years old, on my own with NO MONEY. I had just started one of 3 jobs.

I sold my crappy van for scrap (before my ex came to get it...sabotage was his thing back then).

I started my new life with 150 dollars, NO WHEELS, and only the love of my kids and the confidence my parents instilled in me.

WTF am I even doing? was a constant whisper in my ear.

How did I do it? I remember it so vividly.

I survived on protein shakes, Tostitos, and strawberries.

WTF am I even doing?

I had zero clue. I waitressed, worked retail, and, WAIT FOR IT...

I online dated for sport.

It kept me company on the other side of shame.

Dating became a distraction from my feelings of failure. PLUS, I was really good at it! Who knew?

I married my first boyfriend. WAS I A PRO DATER?

I have brothers, uncles, and a dad I adored. I knew not to give anything away for free (remember the cow?), and so it went.

I had a KILLER dating profile.

It was all adrenaline, all the time.

Was I sad often? HELL YES!

Did I know WTF I was even doing? NEVER!

I would go home after work and cruise dating sites like it was my calling.

Eharmony, Plenty of Fish, OK Cupid, Match. I was a MAESTRO.

I wasn't searching for desert island compatibility. My criteria were simple. If they had a nice smile, a cool occupation, and lived in a place I'd like to visit, I would be in touch.

BONUS POINTS: A guy with a great body and a boat was my holy grail. Stick around to see if I find both.

My line was, "Hello there, I'm intrigued by your (insert anything here). TELL ME MORE, PRETTY PLEASE!" It worked every time!

It was always *another weekend, another guy.* I was so afraid of being alone with my thoughts that I would leave a dinner date with one guy for a sunset stroll with another.

Sure, there were some creeps, countless dick pics, and times I wanted to chew my arm off BEFORE the appetizers, but my male influences trained me well.

A simple "You've got the wrong girl" was the only armour I needed. WHY LIE WHEN THE TRUTH WILL DO?

A cocktail of adrenaline and cortisol kept me high on life.

There were COUNTLESS dates, MANY sunset sails, fireside chats, heart-soul connections, and moonlit moments that soothed my soul. The laughter was like medicine healing me one heartfelt memory at a time.

If I felt disconnected, I would dial up a date.

It was a sport for me and WAY cheaper than therapy...but I had that too!

Segue to me needing a car and having to get a real job to make real money.

I heard about a job opportunity soon after. I was at a Halloween party dressed as a dirty nurse. Don't hate the player, hate the game...

I was good at it. UBER GOOD.

And so it went. On January 1, 2013, I took my show on the road selling advertising North America wide...but not before I rode shotgun to Florida with a guy 20 years my senior to stay in a separate wing in his beach villa. That was my 48-hour stint as a TROPHY WIFE.

I was there to look good, hold the mic while he sang karaoke, and walk his dog. If ONLY that dog could talk.

It was the perfect prelude to my next two years of international dating just for the fun of it.

By the way, you can be assured for many reasons (too many to list) that this was the best scenario for the kids.

WTF am I even doing? I still did NOT have an effing clue!

But the sun rose every morning, and that was always a great start.

I flew straight from Naples, Florida, to Duluth, Minnesota. I thought for sure I'd need a sealskin parka to weather the cold, but subzero temps were the least of my concerns. I HAD BIGGER PROBLEMS.

There I was...BROKE at arrivals in Duluth, my ONLY chance at making money starting in one hour, and NO IDEA how to sell advertising.

WTF am I even doing? I thought. How hard could it be?

Turns out, it was my genius zone. Not only was I born to date, but I was also BORN TO SELL.

I can hear my parents now OOZING with pride. *Lisa's amazing at advertising sales AND dating for sport.*

Does it seem like the Sleaze factor was on FULL TILT? Uh-huh, honey. But that's not how it went. Nope. NOT AT ALL!

As it turns out, I loved advertising and was good at it for all the right reasons. Competing during the day and in between dates for dollars was a playing field I hadn't enjoyed since high school sports as a kid. My confidence was restored quickly.

WTF am I even doing?

I didn't know, but DAMMIT it was a blast! Just not always.

There I was, life on the open road…

GLAMOUROUS, they said!
MYSTERIOUS, they said.
YOU LUCKY DUCK, they said.

To give context, the saying goes that you either DRINK, F*CK, or GAMBLE to survive on the road.

I chose none of the above and instead invented a thing I called "detached dating" to keep me thriving while surviving.

I developed dating into an ART FORM. It distracted me from my demons. It was a survival mechanism that I managed to make FUN.

I was in a different place every ten days and spent more time in airports, hotels, and rental cars than I did at home. My demons and I fit perfectly in my carry-on luggage, and in the middle of all the men and travel mayhem, I found myself — and my way back to my kids, my heart, and my home.

I was on the road so much, even the truckers thought I was a trucker.

Before we begin this next part, I should note that:

Not knowing *WTF I am even doing* is a theme with me. I say YES anyway. I GO anyway. In most cases, I take the trip, and I buy the t-shirt before I know where to go.

And so it began...I was on the move, and I've NEVER been so magnetic. I proved I could manifest men ANYWHERE, and I did.

This sagebrush soul medicated her solo status with dates.

It was RAINING MEN wherever I went.

This is the perfect time to emphasize (although my girlfriends disagree) that I JUST dated. That's it. I didn't "hook up" (well, hardly ever).

True story. It's an energetic standard thing. I was raised right, remember?

There were a few of particular note. It's really hard for me NOT to give you every juicy detail.

BUT! Suffice it to say...

You can IMAGINE THE REST and fill in the blanks...

I behaved badly...you know, the good kind of bad. Gutsy, just shy of stupidity? I rode that line WELL.

It was the BEST of times and the WORST of times. HOP ABOARD. Come along for the ride. This is MY TRIP, but I adore a great winger.

I may list too many, but it's important that you understand the MAGNITUDE of the myriad of men I met on my mission to find myself.

The dates were plentiful, and they all took me one step closer to getting back to myself. Each guy had a sordid story. I shed my shroud of shame and eventually found my way home to the woman and mother that knew I was.

BUCKLE UP, here we go. Some dates of note in no particular order are:

There was the Irish Catholic Bostonian preppy that told me he was addicted to porn, right after he told me his best friend was his sister, who was A NUN...all before dinner was served. ARE YOU KIDDING ME?

There was the hot tub & pool guy (he had both) that was a Sales Pro turned SWINGER. You do WHAT on weekends?

There was Pretty Boy. This guy had the audacity to equate me baking him cookies with an invitation for his c*ck. I'm still curious as to how that economy works.

There was Frenchy...how do you say "GET ME THE HELL OUTTA HERE" in French? Eeeeeewwww! If I had a dollar for how many times he told me he was good in the sack...

There was Larry, the NFL referee (what was I thinking? A REF? Come on!). SO BORING! I left halfway through dinner. Rude, I know, but it had to happen. He was SUCH A BLOWHARD! Wow. That's a good ref joke!

Larry Part 2...I left halfway through dinner because I met a guy at the bar that had tickets to the Stanley Cup finals that night. Of course, I said HELL YA! Yes, Grandma...I stayed safe!

The guy that lived in the hotel RIGHT BESIDE the prison...really? I PASSED on his day pass.

Then Peter Pan, a tenured professor from U of V whose par view was chewing tobacco and talking dirty to his students. THEY PAY

YOU FOR THIS?

There was the married roller skating champ turned insurance salesman from Texas that said his wife ok'd his extracurricular girls. INSERT EYE ROLL HERE.

There was the Orange heli pilot that drove from DC to PA because he thought I'd ENJOY one of his world-famous massages. Is THAT what they call it in DC?

There was the Fox News anchor from Memphis (it's true, Fox is fake)...seriously, he was FAKE NEWS. CATFISH fake. Real talk!

There was the fireman and his abs. OH, THOSE ABS. He wanted me to sleep with his wife AND him. I'm the perfect UNICORN, they said. Google it. I had to!

There was the truck driver Olympian (it's a real-life event) that took me on a Tom Sawyer-esque boating weekend to Lake of the Ozarks and was so impaired he got lost...so I lost HIM.

There was the Gynecologist from the UK that specialized in real-life vaginal rejuvenation. He wasn't a big talker but DID I CARE? Curiosity killed the cat with him. I couldn't stay a NUN forever, although it was quite BIBLICAL in proportion!

Then a definite fave was the like-minded Libra boat captain who wore a life jacket on our date because he couldn't swim. It was one of the BEST dates EVER. He lost the keys. The engine broke down. He had me lean TITANIC STYLE over the bow to grab the buoy we lost...around and around we went. BEST game of "Have You Ever" EVER!

It wasn't ALL kissing frogs. They weren't ALL train wrecks. Most were magical nights of fun and frolic...all jewels in my self-discovery crown.

There were 2 REAL contenders! I actually gave these two a second look.

Mr. T. Virginia. The T stands for TESTOSTERONE. He is a heli pilot, VMI grad, 2x Iraq tours, engineer, cowboy with a homestead on the Jackson River. ALL TRUE. He was in the lead until he promised me posh OVER and OVER, and I got Perkins Restaurant instead. He made Moonshine and ate squirrel. Apparently, it's great with raisin gravy! Need I say more?

WTF am I even doing? I thought. I'll try ONE more time.

Queue Mr. T. Justice, Denver (you get the T). He is a judge, owns a school, is a coach, a jock, and he ran for Senate. He was THE REAL DEAL. I Googled him. He met me at the airport with jewellery and flowers, and we headed off to salsa dance ALL night. He checked ALL the boxes. ALL of them. I mean A L L of them…plus, he was only a 38 dollar Spirit return flight away. Things were looking up.

PLOT TWIST. It was weekend number 2. He surprised me at the airport with his one-year-old LOVE CHILD from a one-night stand. While he coached, I pushed this baby around, thinking *WTF am I even doing?* This is TOO MUCH, even for me. Asking me to caretake was like asking Beyoncé to sing back up.

Fast forward to…in sales what they call THE DEAL BREAKER. Since I was so good at sales, he asked me if I would be able to sell his school bus (yes, all the cool guys have one) AND his grand piano to get cash for his daughter's tuition. His moonlight gig at the Quickstop just wasn't enough. I CAN'T make this stuff up. Guess what? I sold BOTH before noon with HIS BABY in my arms. As it turns out, buses and pianos are commodities in Denver. WHO KNEW? He called me Wonder Woman (I WAS) and wanted me to call him Batman. It was SO MUCH FUN until it wasn't.

Follow the bouncing ball. Connect the dots. This was my life then. No one could keep that pace, not even me. Again, this is only a peek. There is a JUICY book in between the lines.

It was WTF moment after WTF moment, and you know what? It was WORTH IT!

Indeed, dopamine and distraction aren't all they are cracked up to be. Dopamine and distraction only carry you until you can't even hide from yourself...even in your OWN mind.

So many men, so little time...I did ALL OF THAT just to figure out I like cowboys better than lumberjacks?

WTF am I even doing?

I began to question WHY. Yes, sh*t got existential all of a sudden.

How, in the middle of masking my misery with ALL of those men and travel mayhem, did I manage to find myself?

I don't quite know. I JUST DID.

Every WTF am I even doing? moment fuelled my next move.

I was surrounded by people. I couldn't stand still. It was fun, but the scenario was CHAOS by normal standards.

Sure,

There were the MEN...

There were the STORIES...

The SPA TRIPS...

The BOUTIQUE SHOPPING...

The HOTELS...

The CITIES...

The NEW FRONTIERS...

The OPENING NIGHTS...

The OPERA...

The BOX SEATS...

The DRIVERS TO AND FRO...

The BACKSTAGE PASSES...

But there were infinite nights alone full of quiet contemplation with myself...where shedding my skin was non-negotiable, and I was forced to reconcile and get granular about my cold, harsh reality.

At a glance, it looked like I was thriving. The blunt truth was that I was made for life on the road because I could be whomever I wanted wherever I went. No one needed to hear my story of shame. Sale by sale, mile by mile, date by date, I could almost fool myself into believing that my story read differently than it did.

I had NO home.
I had LITTLE contact with my kids.
I had ZERO meaningful commitments, and I liked it that way.
I LOST MYSELF because I gave up on her a LONG time ago.

ME. The pony they call wildfire. ALL ALONE, shrouded in shame with my darkened past. My future was DARKENING day by day.

WTF am I even doing to my kids?

And so it went. I took a GOOD HARD look.

WTF am I even doing running away?
HEALING, that's what.
FORGIVING MYSELF, that's what.
BELIEVING IN MYSELF AGAIN, that's what.

Through it all, I led with LOVE, because LOVE WINS.

QUEUE MUSIC, please...
I got a new job (close to home).
I got a place of my own (it felt so good).
I got real that I was running from anything real in my life (demons demolished).
I got RECONNECTED WITH MY KIDS (they are inspiring, independent, self-cleaning ovens).

DRUM ROLL, please. I got a guy. I call him Cowboy. He's my RIDE OR DIE. He has a boat AND a hot body, hates squirrels, and loves to WTF (every day is a trip with him!).

I miss the road. But I love HOME in a way I haven't in years.

I love ME in a way I haven't in...EVER!

Do I know *WTF am I even doing?* Not often.

That part of me WON'T change — and frankly, I hope it NEVER does. I'm grateful for my messiness. It's given me mastery. **It's in NOT KNOWING that life gets rich.**

It's in the WTF MESSY MASTERY in between knowing and not knowing that life gets juicy, the lessons get large, and the love gets LARGER.

Let me say it again. Listen closely. THE LOVE GETS LARGER, and so does life!

As long as I live and breathe, I won't know *WTF I am even doing* the majority of the time. I say that's A BEAUTIFUL THING!

The magic in life MAGNIFIES while we EMBRACE the messy mystery of life.

My mantra now? Get MESSY. Ask, *WTF?* Make MAGIC!

If I'm not *WTFing* am I really even ALIVE?

CHAPTER 12

Monika Amber

@NURTURINGNATURALLYEO

HTTPS://MONIKAAMBER.WIXSITE.COM/NURTURINGNATURALLYEO

"**Y**ou are a hypocrite!" This was a message I received after painfully revealing that I was going through a divorce and was now a single mom to four daughters.

The message came from a woman who only months before had thanked me for the online marriage course I had run a few years prior that gave her the skills she needed to help save her marriage. It was a course in which I thought I was transparent enough that they knew I was not running it because I had it all together, but because I needed it as much as they did.

Yet here I was, staring at the message, adding insult to injury.

No one goes into marriage thinking it is going to end. No one walks into motherhood thinking. *One day I am going to do this ALL ALONE!* If that's what we foresaw, WE WOULDN'T FREAKING SIGN UP FOR IT, would we?!?!

But here I was, being called a hypocrite.
Should I wear that title?
Do I give it weight?
At first, I did.
At first, I wasn't healed enough to see that I was so much more than that.

Isn't that the tricky thing about motherhood? Trauma? Recovery?
We lose ourselves.
We forget who we are and how we were designed.
We are so consumed by everyone else's thoughts, opinions, and unsolicited advice.
We get lost.

I was only 19 when I said "I do."
I had walked through a lot of trauma before that day.
By stepping into marriage and then quickly becoming a mom, I never really had a chance to find out who I was. I never had the opportunity to walk through healing.
So I brought it all with me.
The pain.
The hurt.
The weight (physically and emotionally) came into mommyhood with me.

Most moms are ecstatic when they find out they are expecting.
What I felt resembled shock. Early on, when dating D.C. he informed me he could not have children due to a health issue, so we never tried to prevent anything.
But, lo and behold, 6 months into marriage, my 20-year-old self

was PREGNANT!

Prior to discovering that I was pregnant, I had already battled
thoughts that getting married may have been a mistake.
I was young. I had so much unresolved trauma. The timing was
rushed. I needed out!
Could I get the marriage annulled at this point?
Would that be best?
So the unexpected pregnancy added to the shock and heaviness of
it all.

Don't get me wrong, I always felt like I was born to be a mom...but
I bounced between excitement and dread, because now that I was
going to be a mother, in my mind this also meant I was going to
be stuck in this marriage.
Stuck.
It was a feeling that would stay with me for the next decade.

Someone once told me that birth was the most beautiful thing.
I watched a video in prenatal class...there was nothing beautiful
about it. However, I held optimism that my birth would indeed be
beautiful — because I had a plan.

None of it worked out.
My plan was useless.
Want to know what I did not plan?
A broken tailbone.
I also had a student use what I SWEAR was a crochet hook to
break my water, and then, geez...if you ever THINK your water
has broken, I assure you it has NOT.
You will know for a fact when it has. There is no "thinking" it
happened. When the Red Sea comes at full force, THEN, my
friend, you know your water has broken.
You know those pads they tell you to buy postpartum? Why does
NO ONE tell you that the ones the size of a houseboat are where

it's at?

No, there was nothing beautiful about it.

But my baby...my baby was *marvelous.*
At that moment, I grew up.
I gave myself to someone else to hold for life.
Changed.
Transformed.
Complete.
That part was beautiful.

Then came the postpartum depression.
Some people call it the "baby blues."
They say every mom gets it.
Yet, as someone who battled with mental wellness from a young age, no one warned me how terribly strong it could wash over you. It had the power to make all those wonderful moments you felt holding that baby for the first time mean nothing, because you felt like you were nothing.
That's when you start to fully lose yourself.

I got to such a horrible place that I needed my friend to come and take my baby and bring me to the hospital to get help.
But if you looked at me, you never would have guessed.
I always looked like I had it all together.
I was the "Pinterest-perfect Mom" before that was even a thing.
Under that surface, that delicate shell, I held all my broken pieces that didn't know where they belonged.

Not long after that, I was expecting again.
Early on in that pregnancy, I was working three jobs. One of them was running an in-home childcare where I took care of a handful of tiny tots, including a beautiful young boy with a mitochondrial disease. This left me carrying him up and down our multilevel home several times a day. Eventually, my body couldn't take it

anymore. It was too much, and I had to walk away.

That broke me.

I loved him so much, but I also knew it was best for all the children involved if I stepped away.

During that time, our financial strain deepened because D.C. also underwent a drastic life-saving health procedure. This left him without work and with little to no immune system.

And me? It left me with no space or time to properly grieve and adapt to this huge life change.

So there I was, doing my best to hold all those pieces together, but in reality I was falling apart.

After giving birth to my second wonderful daughter, I was left feeling utterly hopeless.

My marriage was in shambles.

My stress was through the roof.

Financially, we were drowning.

Once again, a wave of depression flooded my life.

This one, however, flared ALL my borderline personality disorder tendencies and the eating disorder that I had battled for so long.

These issues raised their ugly heads.

I quickly lost 65 lbs, and while everyone celebrated my external victories, no one saw the truth of what got me there.

It was great because behind that veil, I could hide the binging and purging, the starving myself, the suicidal tendencies, and the cutting — the deep, ugly cuts made by my own hand.

I would watch it bleed just to try and see if the internal pain could be matched externally.

It didn't help.

We decided what would save our marriage was to move since having another baby didn't do the trick.

So we moved...

...Away from everyone I knew.

...Away from the home I had created.

...Away from the safety net that surrounded me.

We moved to a disgusting hole-in-the-wall house that, in hindsight, was really a pinnacle piece in the demise of my marriage. When I walked into the house, what I felt was that I didn't matter. I was not enough.

I was unworthy of anything more than a mould-infested, nicotine-dripping, ceiling crumbled on the floor house. It was never a home.

I struggled — emotionally, physically, and financially.

However, my mask and my walls got bigger and better.

No one saw how hard I had to work to hold it all together.

Let me paint you a picture of the remainder of our relationship.

Two more babies.

A foot broken in 7 places.

Unbelievable health scares.

11 basement floods.

Broken furnaces.

Hospital visit after hospital visit.

Research, endless research.

Fighting for my daughter's health and life on multiple occasions.

Homeschooling.

Volunteering.

Running and organizing church and community groups.

Starting my own business.

I did it all.

Everyone thought I was a superwoman.

I let them think that.

But underneath it all, below the surface and survival cocktail I had mixed up, I was broken and drowning.

When would enough be enough?

What am I even doing?!
I know.
Let's move again.
THAT will solve EVERYTHING!
But this time, it kind of did.

Let me be clear, moving didn't end my marriage.
It didn't change me.
But if we hadn't moved, I truly do not think I would still be alive.
Maybe that sounds like I'm exaggerating. But I know me. I know
how deep the hurt and pain were. I know how trapped and helpless
I felt, living in toxicity and hiding my pain.

I wanted my children to be enough.

They are everything.
Incredible.
Beautiful.
My heartbeat.

But when toxicity washes over you from every corner, sometimes
it isn't enough to save you. If we hadn't moved, I don't know if my
mental health would have survived. I had to see that I was worth so
much more than all of this hell. I had to be able to look at that girl in
the mirror and think, *YOU ARE VALUABLE! YOU ARE WORTHY!*
This is NOT how you were designed! I had to see myself as more
than "just" a wife and mother.

So I poured myself into my business with passion, and as my business grew, I learned to dive deep into my blocks, identifying the
broken pieces and festering wounds that needed healing. When you
are working for yourself, you are the only one getting in your way!

So I had to learn to get out of my own way.
I had never spent much time travelling — in fact, I had only been
on a plane once before.

Yet I had the opportunity to start travelling for business.
I started discovering who I was.
I began healing those broken pieces of myself.
With all of that came the realization that I couldn't stay in this.
I could not be "that girl" anymore.
What kind of example was I showing my four incredible daughters?

My head and my heart needed to start communicating with each other, not blocking each other.
Travelling and teaching were the best decisions I ever made because they led me to myself.
I found *me*.
I was broken and hurting, but I saw myself for the first time in many years.

I never could have anticipated that going to San Diego, California would be life-changing.
But it was, and it all happened in a moment and in a way I never foresaw.

Have you ever had this feeling, like a whisper in your soul that you can't seem to shake? That's what this was. I had just had the most incredible business achievement to date and was recognized in front of a crowd filled with my mentors, friends, and my company's elite. As I walked across that stage, they were all there cheering for me. Within moments of it happening, D.C completely destroyed that incredible moment for me. He was the one person in the world that should have believed in me the most, had my back, and was my biggest cheerleader. Instead, from half a continent away via text message, he took that all away from me. Between walking off that stage and arriving back at my seat, my whole world shifted because of it.

I broke.

In that brokenness came a feeling, a whisper to my soul that was so strong. It whispered, *"Go down the boardwalk, find the Pacific Ocean, and run into it."* I mean, it is California, the land of fun and sun. This should have been something I was more than happy to do. But the truth is, it was March, and the weather was more jeans-and-t-shirt weather, not swimming-in-the-ocean weather. Plus, it was getting dark, and who in their right mind goes down to the ocean in the dark? Yet, I couldn't shake it. I needed to go. I needed to listen to that voice.

So I looked at my friends and said, "Ladies, wanna adventure with me?" They agreed, and soon, the three of us were unexpectedly heading out to face a moment that would change my life forever.

There, on the horizon in the setting sun, lay the beautiful Pacific Ocean.

Once we got to the edge of the ocean I said to my friends, "I need to go in the water." I took off my shoes and made my way across the sand, jeans and all. My walk quickly turned to a jog and then a run as I made my way to the ocean's edge.

I timidly placed my feet in the water and closed my eyes and raised my hands in surrender to God. At the moment my arms were fully extended, a song was immediately placed on my heart. With eyes closed tightly and arms fully raised, I sang these words that flowed through me with all the passion and gusto and tears stored up inside of me.

"Here I am, broken and failing. Here I am, falling apart. Here I am, hurting and sad, waiting for Your loving arms to hold me close. I am here, torn, and shattered, I am here, but it's not enough. I am here, hurting, unworthy, longing to feel like I am loved. And there You are holding me closely. There You are shielding me in your arms. You are here whispering my name, telling me I'm worthy. Release me from harm. Because I am enough. I am enough. I am enough."

As the last, *"I am enough"* slipped from my lips, a huge wave came in and washed over me. In that wave, I heard the words *"I release you."* That was the moment I knew my marriage was over and that I was going to be okay.

Once I arrived home, the reality of that moment and all that it meant started to sink in. What you need to understand is that over the course of seven years, he threatened to leave me seventeen times. Yes, I counted.

In order to process this reality before facing him, I checked myself into a hotel and spent an entire day thinking and praying about how to proceed with this "ocean moment" realization. I decided during that time that I would try to make my marriage work for another 6 months.

That was my plan when I got home.
The caveat was that if he tells me he is leaving, I won't fight him to stay this time.

Less than 24 hours after being home, I got a text message from the other room.
The gist of the message was, "I am done."
My response: "Ok, then go."

When you suddenly step into life as a single mom, you feel a lot of things.
Failure is definitely high on that list.
How do you breathe? Cope? Walk through this with the children? What if they hate me?

It's so hard to think that you can go from a place of feeling like you are drowning and wondering *what am I doing?* to a place of knowing you are doing the right thing and that you are worthy and valuable enough to push through. But you absolutely can. I know because I have lived on both sides. And I hope the lessons I have learned will bring you hope that you can too.

The biggest thing I learned from walking my children through the pain of divorce is to be an example of a force, a strength, a beacon of light in dark places. Pain can teach us powerful lessons. Use these lessons as an example to your children that in the midst of the storm, you can find yourself.

Choose yourself.
It doesn't make you selfish.
You can be angry.
Cry.
Laugh.
Dance it out.
Sing too loud.
Through the pain and the lessons, you can find your power.

As parents, we want to protect our children from battling the way we have battled, but maybe our job is to fight our own battle well and then help give them the tools and the armour to fight when their turn comes.

I want to raise strong, resilient children who will be world-changers, voices for the voiceless, people with conviction and compassion.

How can I raise children like that if I am not first a woman like that?

Finding myself has truly helped me grow as a mother. I am no longer establishing standards and expectations I cannot first uphold myself.

I've learned so much from my pain, and that pain has taught me that I need to leave room and create space for my children to do the same. I began to realize that as I healed, I was teaching my children that to love someone well meant they needed to first love themselves.

No more diminishing or shrinking.

It has to be about seeing your child as they are, not as a reflection of your own insecurities.

Acknowledge that failure is central to greatness and is necessary to succeed.

Break the cycle of needing to be valued by others at the expense of your own self-worth.

Plow through the challenges together.

Your children will be strong for it, and your relationships will thrive — certainly with the victories, but even in the losses.

We do not have permission to work out our junk on the beautiful blank canvases of our children.

In order to raise a strong woman, we have to be able to recognize one.

In order to recognize one, we need to give ourselves permission to be one.

Being a whole woman is at the very heart of it.

So, go be whole.

Even if it's scary and you have no idea what on Earth you are doing.

Choose you.

Choose to take ONE small step at a time.

Understand that NO ONE knows what they are doing — they simply decided to journey towards wholeness.

CHAPTER 13

Niki Bechtloff

PHOTO: **HEATHER BLACKWELL PHOTOGRAPHY**

We descended a staircase of twisted tree roots until we saw the ocean lapping against the shore. We found the nearest stump, which was toppled on its side, and set up our picnic. The crisp September air danced around us as we eagerly watched for some type of spiritual sign. My daughter was nestled in between my husband and me, her warmth radiating against us. She was the first to notice a large bald eagle soaring overhead. Tears fell, waiting to be picked up by the next wave as we reflected on this moment. We imagined coming to this beach as a family of four to celebrate the birth of our baby boy. Instead, we commemorated his due date by taking turns holding the tiny urn, rubbing our fingers along the turquoise teddy bear etched into it.

From a young age, I viewed pregnancy as a rite of passage with a predictable outcome. I aspired to be part of the Motherhood club and dreamt about cradling my round belly, feeling carefree and confident. I was barely out of my wedding dress before questions started about growing our family. I enthusiastically answered, fantasizing about when we would have children and how many — foolishly believing I was in control.

The pregnancy test revealed the eagerly anticipated result — *Pregnant*. I had gained entry into this elusive group. I was elated, ecstatic, and a little bit nauseous, but I had made it. Immediately, the advice poured in about what to eat, how to sleep, and how to navigate the journey. I read the books and consumed the information sent my way with the expectation of a fairytale outcome.

For those that successfully navigate pregnancy and delivery, the rules are simple. You are united and entitled to share intimate details about morning sickness, body changes, food aversions, and delivery woes. These collective experiences are your badges of honour. Maybe I was naive in my pursuit of becoming a mother, or maybe I simply believed the narrative that was fed to me my entire life. I wholeheartedly embraced the notion that if I followed all of the guidelines, I would embody motherhood as advertised. I envisioned my future family — two children with a two-year age gap. I imagined sharing their birth stories, smiling as we reminisced. Instead, I found myself in uncharted waters, overwhelmed by feelings of failure and isolation.

While we listen intently to the celebratory recollections, we avoid the painful stories about abortions, miscarriages, and early inductions — the losses, the *What the Fuck* moments that make others uncomfortable and leave us scarred and alone. This is where you'll find me, orbiting the club that I desperately wanted to be part of. Instead of enjoying Mars bars and milkshakes, I was given misoprostol and morphine.

My first pregnancy exposed me to soft markers, genetic testing, and an emergency Caesarean section at 35 weeks gestation. As we sat in the small office waiting for our obstetrician, we could hear as she finished up with another expectant mom. The static sound of a baby's heartbeat vibrated through the wall. Our door swung open, and her demeanour noticeably changed as she entered. She placed the doppler in her oversized coat pocket, sat on her stool, and folded her hands on her lap before speaking. I tried to escape her gaze, but she held eye contact while reluctantly mentioning the words *Trisomy 18*. She offered reassurances but also informed us that she was obligated to report her findings since our daughter had several markers on her anatomy scan.

I quickly obtained my schooling in pregnancy complications from the countless medical appointments accompanied by endless hours scouring the internet.

During our next appointment, we sat in the same places, nervously awaiting the update. The noninvasive genetic test revealed that our daughter had a very low risk of Trisomy 18. The odds were in our favour, but I still felt like the deck was stacked against us.

Due to a single umbilical artery, I was sent for regular ultrasounds to monitor her growth. As a first-time mom, I felt fortunate to have multiple ultrasounds, watching as she frolicked and sucked her thumb. I was 32 weeks pregnant when the technician politely excused herself to check on the quality of the photos. I leapt from the bed to search for my phone while simultaneously trying to steal glances of the grainy images on the monitor. I sent a message to my husband to notify him that something was wrong. As the message sent, she returned to the room along with a radiologist who adjusted her glasses and directed the technician to capture new images. She rested her hand genially on the technician's shoulder, a subtle congratulation on her finding. Our daughter had developed an aneurysm where the umbilical cord was inserted into the placenta.

This abnormality sent us to a high-risk hospital where a team of specialists balanced the aneurysm risks with the goal of carrying my baby closer to term. I found comfort at these regular appointments in the dimly lit room, listening as the technician captured the rhythmic sound of blood rushing through her middle cerebral artery. Later, I would learn these findings would become a pivotal factor in deciding to deliver her early. As we sat surrounded by the humming of machines, we were informed that our daughter's organs were struggling to function. Stoically, I stared ahead, numbed by the constant irregular findings.

We consulted with obstetricians and fetal medicine specialists until they reached a consensus that it was best to deliver her the following day. After all of the worry and risks of a premature birth, she defied the odds. My arms enveloped her tiny 5-pound body, amazed she was here. I revelled in this victory, reminding myself that despite the complications, she made it.

Armed with multiple reassurances from genetic counsellors and therapists, we felt ready to try for our second baby. Our daughter would be four years old, and although it wasn't the age gap we originally anticipated, we were grateful to be in a position to move forward both emotionally and physically. Our daughter napped as we paced around the bathroom, waiting for the test result. *Pregnant..* even though we were excited, we were conflicted with both hope and fear. We understood the complexities of this process and knew it wasn't to be taken lightly.

I found myself holding my belly, nervously protecting it, as I reacquainted myself with what I needed to do to support a healthy pregnancy. During my 8-week ultrasound, my discomfort and fears came rushing back. I carefully watched the technician as she navigated the murky waters. My eyes stung, but I was unable to blink as I worried about an adverse finding. She sighed in frustration on more than one occasion but wouldn't divulge any information. She pressed firmly into my abdomen before letting me know that my retroverted uterus was making the scan difficult. As she prepared for an internal ultrasound, she discussed the process, not knowing that I was well versed with it. The wand burned as it was inserted, and I held my breath until her shoulders relaxed, an unconscious signal that she had found the heartbeat. A small black bubble encased by a larger one appeared on the screen. The shadowy figure didn't resemble a baby yet, and deep down, I felt like it never would.

Unaware of my anxiety, she removed the tool and noted that the heartbeat was strong. She quickly cleaned her workstation to prepare for her next patient. She passed the sonogram across the bed as I used my shirt to wipe up the remaining gel. I studied the picture, searching for any clues to signal something was wrong.

I clenched the paper and fought back the urge to cry as I approached my car. My husband and daughter leaned forward in their seats, giddy for an update. Tears streamed down my cheeks, and I watched the colour drain from my husband's face. I choked on the tears as I sobbed, "I know something is wrong."

Before my next prenatal appointment, I prepared for the worst, but my doctor assured me that despite a small but very normal bleed, everything looked normal. She rechecked the ultrasound notes and swivelled around from her computer desk to remind me that it would be very unlikely for something to go wrong. I followed her advice and found myself enjoying the next 9 weeks. It became easier to remind myself that my nervousness stemmed from the emotional toll of my first pregnancy along with a recent move to a new province. It was a move that left us isolated from our family. My stomach continued to grow, and my all-day sickness reminded me that everything was progressing.

Easter approached, and we decided to travel to Ontario to spend time with family. As we made the social rounds, I began to notice a dull ache in my abdomen. Anxiety drove me to the hospital as I desperately searched for reassurance. My heart raced as I watched fleeting images reflect off the technician's glasses. The silence dissipated as my husband questioned if she was doing a full anatomy scan. We reminded her our anatomy scan was booked for the following week when we returned to British Columbia. Her eyes didn't leave the screen as she typed notes and captured more pictures. I looked at my husband, signalling defeat, each of us acknowledging that this appointment was not going well.

Her voice broke as she asked if we wanted to know the sex of our baby. We nodded reluctantly, and she stripped off her gloves before confirming it was a boy. I replayed her facial features and tone. After our daughter's high-risk pregnancy, we became in tune with slight inflections, trembling voices, and vacant stares. Every technician, nurse, and physician we encountered all shared the same look. It was a look that was filled with discomfort and guilt — guilt that came from knowing that we would soon receive life-changing information.

I crumpled the paper sheet and got dressed, yet I felt more exposed than ever. She cleared her throat and told us that we needed to meet with the doctor right away. We nodded as we studied the picture. Something was wrong. His facial features blurred together, and large black pockets appeared on his abdomen and chest.

She turned on the light as she left the room. I sat on my hands and crossed my legs to keep myself from coming apart. The familiar feeling of heartache crept in as we walked towards our meeting with the doctor. We sat on hard plastic chairs while we waited for him to speak with us. He was hunched over the nurse's station, fanning through a stack of papers. He paced around the desk, rechecking his file before stopping to make a few phone calls. His discomfort was palpable. The reception area was empty except for us, and he froze when he noticed us. He rubbed his eyes, pressed his hands along his white jacket, and shuffled our papers as neatly as possible back into the folder.

The thudding of my heart could be heard and felt all over my body as I sat in his large sterile office. It had one window, and the dreary day crept in. The office had an awkward layout with an exam table in the middle of the room. A small Tudor desk was tucked away in the corner with more uncomfortable plastic chairs jammed around it. It was set up for examinations and felt too big for our conversation. However, the walls caved in on us as he began to share the ultrasound findings. Suddenly his oversized space became too small for the gravity of our situation.

There was a reverent silence as the doctor repeated the words *Trisomy 13*. Five syllables reverberated in my mind, eviscerating me as I tried to remember which chapter this was from. He spoke in a monotone voice as if he was reading from a script, barely looking up to see if we were digesting the information. The words echoed around us, followed by his recommendation for an immediate delivery. I choked on the prognosis as I tried to repeat his instructions. He replied flatly, making it abundantly clear that my pregnancy was not viable.

Trisomy 13, also known as Patau's Syndrome, is a chromosomal disorder. It's a rare diagnosis that can lead to insurmountable birth defects, impacting nearly every organ. Without hesitation, the doctor indicated that our son was unlikely to survive to term in our situation. If we continued with the pregnancy, he would not survive delivery. We met with specialists, and they too guided us to pregnancy termination. I cringed as they repeated that the safest option was an induced abortion. I was halfway through my pregnancy and couldn't grasp that this was my situation. They reiterated their recommendation but allowed us to question and explore further.

Equipped with this devastating information, we knew time was not on our side. We spent the next few days meeting with genetic counsellors and specialists while continuing to research. Information was abundant but not in a manner that could be consumed by a grief-stricken family. The words blurred, conversations were fuzzy, and articles on the internet gave us a false sense of hope.

In addition to multiple ultrasounds and medical opinions, we also requested an amniocentesis to provide us with unwavering certainty of the diagnosis. The waiting room for the procedure was crowded as people anxiously gathered before their names were called. A nurse appeared and said my name, but my legs turned to stone as I tried to walk forward. A team waited for us and ushered me onto the bed. They worked methodically, simultaneously explaining the procedure and preparing my abdomen, proving this wasn't their first time. I counted the ceiling tiles to distract myself from the information that I couldn't comprehend.

Unlike my other ultrasounds, this time they didn't dim the lights. I watched as my son wiggled across the monitor as they scanned to find the perfect place to insert the needle. The doctor counted slowly, but I felt the needle pierce my abdomen and then my uterus before she made it to the number three. I was thankful she spared me from the final seconds of the countdown. The results confirmed what they had suspected all along, Trisomy 13, but this time it was without a doubt.

A few days later, we arrived at the hospital and made our way to the labour and delivery area. We pushed ourselves to the back of the elevator to make room for the other expectant parents, watching as they nervously but excitedly clutched each other's hands. They giddily made their way to the same destination that we somberly dragged ourselves toward.

We whispered our names at the desk, and the nurse solemnly and apologetically wrapped the hospital bracelet around my wrist. She ushered us through the waiting room, and we kept our eyes down, not wanting to burden the excited families with our sorrow. We were escorted to a room at the end of the hall marked by a blue butterfly to notify staff about the loss of a baby.

They started my labour in the morning by giving me my first dose of misoprostol. I didn't know what to expect or when to ask for pain medication since I had only experienced a Caesarean section. Part of me wanted to feel everything as I felt as though I deserved the indescribable pain. I didn't have to change into a gown, and I curled up on the bed and waited for my next dose of medication. My body started to tremble as my blood pressure plummeted. I shivered uncontrollably. I requested more blankets until they were piled on top of me, and all you could see was my head peeking out. I asked my husband to take a photo. My body was crippled by fear, but I still wanted to commemorate the day my son entered this world, even if it was the same day he left it.

I didn't want my family to come. It felt like an unfair situation to thrust them into. I thought it would be better to be alone, so I could keep my grief to myself. The pain overcame me, acting as a riptide pulling me under. My body was numb as I felt a part of me slipping away. And that's when they showed up. My family, driving from all over, prepared to sleep in their cars if that meant they could be close to me. They entered the room, and unbeknownst to them, they pulled me back to shore.

The contractions came quickly and threaded around my stomach. It felt like a vice grip tightening around my abdomen and heart. Every contraction reminded me that it could be the one to stop his heart. I struggled over to the couch and waited for the morphine. Guttural sobs bellowed from me as I pleaded with them to stop the delivery. The morphine kicked in, and I felt a tidal wave as he was born. Tears streamed down my cheeks as I whispered, "Did it happen?"

The nurses and doctor rushed in, springing into action as they carefully cleaned up his still body. They wrapped him in a knit blanket and delicately placed a small blue hat on his head. They handed me a bracelet with his name on it and set him in my arms. I clenched the bracelet, the beads leaving an indentation in the palm of my hand. "Hi Everett, I'm your Mom," I whispered.

The room was busy but silent. My parents guided me back to my bed as the warmth of their embraces stopped my teeth from chattering. Slowly the nurses retreated, and my parents headed home. As the air became heavy again, my husband's parents emerged, as if our families conspired about how to split their visits.

We took turns holding Everett, studying his tiny features, tenderly embracing his body. I watched as he turned purple, reminding me that our time together was fleeting. A thin layer of translucent skin blanketed his failed organs, preserving his peaceful sleep.

As the sun began to rise, a doctor arrived to let me know that I would have to have a procedure known as a dilation and curettage to remove the placenta. I set Everett in his Dad's hands and transferred myself into the wheelchair. The operating light shone above me, casting a peaceful glow on the room. The team worked swiftly. A doctor held my hand while the others performed the surgery, ripping the last of him from me. Back in our room, we savoured every second and cuddled Everett until we had to say goodbye. We placed him in the hospital bassinet, the warming light remaining off. The juxtaposition of seeing his frail body in the newborn cot felt torturous, one final reminder that this wasn't a typical delivery.

I didn't want to let him go, but his body was cold, and it felt cruel to prolong his departure because I wasn't ready. We begged the nurse to go with him wherever he had to go next. She picked him up and turned away, hiding her face as she cried while we said our last goodbye. I felt like we were grieving wrong. Were we crying too much or not enough? Did we hold on too long or let him slip away too fast? I searched my bag for any remaining clues, any books that had a chapter on what I should do next. I sat in the quiet room, staring at the empty bassinet, wondering how this went so wrong.

As we closed the door behind us, we were reminded of the blue butterfly and its significance to our loss. There's rarely a day that goes by that I don't think about Everett. I'm emotionally and physically scarred, and he will be a part of me forever. As we sit at our beach and watch the tide recede, I'm reminded that there's so much more beneath the surface.

CHAPTER 14

RHIANA BROUCKXON

PHOTO: **MADDY OXENHAM**
@RBROXN

have always been fascinated by learning about mental health and how complex the mind is. Previously, I believed I had a good understanding of my own brain and mental health. As much as I would have liked to think that I would automatically notice that something was wrong with my mental health, my postpartum depression and anxiety really just snuck up on me like a freaking ninja! In retrospect, I can see now that I was struggling in that first year of motherhood, but at the time, I had no idea what the f**k was happening. My emotions were completely out of control. "I wish that I could just be numb." I remember saying to my mom one or two times (or three or four times...I don't even remember how many times) that I "wish I didn't have to feel anything." My body would feel every emotion so intensely that it hurt. For a long time, I thought I just had a hormonal imbalance after giving birth. In my mind, everything would be resolved eventually, and things would "balance out." I just needed to push through, and everything would be fine in a few months, right? Wrong. During my pregnancy, my midwives warned me about the signs of postpartum depression, just like most women today are advised to immediately notify a doctor if they feel a slew of certain symptoms. You know, symptoms like not being able to control your crying for more than a few weeks, sadness, changes in appetite, not enjoying activities you would normally enjoy, etc.

In my case, the feelings I had weren't typical postpartum anxiety or depression symptoms, or at least I wasn't aware of them. I didn't know that postpartum rage was even a thing, but let me tell ya...my rage was out of control. Even the smallest and most innocent things could set me off. I was seriously so angry that it hurt throughout my body. It's hard to explain, but you know when you've just gone through a really difficult breakup, and your emotions are almost too intense for words, when your stomach turns, and your heart is broken? It was like that. Even though this was happening to me, for some reason I could not piece together that something was seriously wrong and that I might need help. In my postpartum journey, I assumed I would never face any mental health issues. In my mind, I just figured it could never and would never happen to me, just as I believed the birth of my son would not result in an emergency C-section. HA! I was so sure that everything would be perfect, shiny, and new as soon as he came out. In reality, I was so exhausted and busy with my brand new baby that I had no time to even think about myself, let alone how I truly felt.

My name is Rhiana. My friends call me Rhi (like the bread). I am a mother of two, and I'm here to tell my story of what brought me to where I am today.

In December 2018, at the age of 26, I had my first child, Nash. Before I became pregnant, I worked a lot, spent all of my free time with friends, and indulged every weekend without a care in the world. In fact, I had only been in my new relationship for 7 months when I got pregnant. I was not a homeowner, and I wasn't married — not that any of that matters in the grand scheme of things, but I thought it was worth mentioning that my sh*t wasn't even close to being together. I wasn't following the typical traditional protocols that other people followed before they had a baby. Nobody I knew had started families yet, and nobody was married. We were all still having fun and partying. Honestly, I didn't know what the f*** I was in for when I got pregnant, but when I found out I was expecting, I was terrified and excited all at once. My pregnancy was as easy as it could have been. I was pregnant alongside my amazing sister-in-law — in fact, we were due within the same week. We both found out we were expecting boys at 20 weeks, which was incredibly exciting! Our parents were ecstatic for the first grandchildren in both families! During this time in my life, I truly felt like everyone around me supported me in every way they could. Even though I didn't have my sh*t together, I was happy with my life.

Let's fast forward to the birth of my son, Nash. Obviously, I'd heard of C-sections prior to giving birth, but was I prepared to possibly have one? Definitely not! The birth was completely fine and all, but I just remember thinking to myself that my experience was going to be amazing, and like the baby would just slide out and I would be happy and energized after the birth experience. Like, what? Pardon? Why did I think that? I can't help but laugh at my past self. If I'd known what was possible, I would have prepared myself a little more.

Anyway, my labour started off like a textbook labour would, with contractions that went from 0-100 over many hours. Once the pain reached the point of "Holy Mother of God," we headed to the hospital (fastest drive I've ever experienced, but it felt like it took forever). When I arrived, the midwife who was checking me in asked, "What type of birth are you having?" and I yelled, "AN EPIDURAL ONE," not realizing that she was asking if it was a water birth or natural birth or something else. She laughed and got me the epidural as fast as she could get the anesthesiologist to the room. The rest of the time was smooth sailing until I ended up getting a C-section because the baby was stuck, and I was not progressing fast enough. I was told that my C-section was a "non-emergency, emergency" C-section. But since my water had broken almost 12 hours prior, they wanted to get him out as soon as possible in order to prevent infection and other complications. It wasn't something I was mentally ready for, and I was a little concerned about it, but I kept telling myself that "it is what it is." I was just ready to have my baby in the safest way possible and enjoy the happiest time of my life. Nash was born at 9 lbs 10 oz within an hour of the decision to proceed with a C-section! As soon as we saw him, we fell in love. I was so happy and relieved to finally have my family that I had been waiting almost 10 months for. We spent the night in the hospital and our families came to visit, along with one of our best friends. What a time to be alive! We were on Cloud 9. I still remember that time with all of those warm and fuzzy feelings.

We spent most of the first few days at home recuperating in bed and cuddling as a family. Family and friends were free to come visit whenever they wanted (COVID who?). My postpartum experience was great for the first 5 days, but then I began to feel off. I was throwing up and feeling feverish and sick, like I was coming down with the flu. My midwife was scheduled to come to our house for an appointment that morning and had noticed that a bandage was still on from my C-section. I wish I had taken a picture of her facial expression at that moment. It was like she knew something was very wrong but trying not to freak out

She asked me why I still had the bandage on, and I explained that I was never given instructions to remove it. I had never had surgery, or another C-section for that matter, and no one told me what to do with it, so I left it. In the hospital before we were discharged, I was told that I could shower with it on and everything...so I did, and sure enough, at 8 days postpartum, I woke up in the morning in a pool (yes, pool) of puss in my bed from my incision *shivers*. I was terrified. I literally thought I was going to die. We rushed to the hospital that morning. I ended up being admitted to the hospital for 4 days on IV antibiotics and a drain leading from my C-section incision to a bag attached to my leg for weeks after the nasty infection that I had contracted. To paint a picture of my experience, imagine being in a hospital room in quarantine. Everyone coming into the room was in full PPE (like COVID style PPE, gowns, masks, face shields, etc.). I wasn't allowed to breastfeed my son, and I only got to see him for one hour per day. It was tragic.

I was so incredibly confused and angry that this was my experience after having a brand new baby. I felt as if I was robbed of that perfect experience that I had envisioned for so long. I was so disappointed and sad that I was experiencing such a rough start to what was supposed to be a perfect time in my life. I was constantly asking myself, *WTF is even happening?* HOWEVER, at that time, I was in survival mode. I had a new baby that I wasn't able to be with for 4 days, and my partner was a brand new dad who had to be able to take care of a newborn all by himself while also trying to work because we were so incredibly broke. I just felt like I could not let myself feel the emotions at the time — I couldn't break because then I knew that it would be harder for me to push through. I have always been this way with emotions or things that are bothering me. I usually just let them build up for a while until my feelings tank is full, and something sets me off, and I blow up. It's not good, but it was what it was at that time.

The months following that incident were absolute hell. I was angry and frustrated 95% of the time. I was extremely reactive towards my partner — I was mean and aggressive. I was mad at him over everything — like literally, everything set me off and into a complete spiral.

This is where I thought I was just experiencing hormonal imbalances and that things would just even out. I ended up dealing with this incredibly uncomfortable situation for ten months before I snapped. I remember that night so vividly and clearly. I was completely exhausted and ready to throw in the towel with the life I was living. I was having some extremely dark thoughts and knew that I needed help. I knew that I was not getting better. It was time for me to seek help, which I did. I went on medication for a while, and it helped a bit.

Thankfully, my partner was so incredibly understanding, and it was almost easier to deal with because I knew that it was something that I could fix with the right tools. Soon after, I was diagnosed with General Anxiety Disorder (GAD) and Postpartum Depression. I was relieved when I was diagnosed. I finally felt like I had an answer, and I was eager to start feeling better. To this day, I am in therapy. I am constantly working on my mental health. I have adopted self-care as an incredibly important part of my life. I have things that I care about aside from being a mom, fiancé, dog mom, cleaner, cook, etc. I have made a point to do the things that are challenging and require more thought so that I don't get stuck in a rut. I have learned so much about myself in the past few years than I have ever known about myself. Although my parenting journey started off rocky and I had so many *WTF am I even doing?* moments, I have come to learn that sometimes life throws you a curveball, and you just have to learn how to roll with it and figure out how to keep moving forward.

The craziest part of this whole thing was that no one knew that I was struggling except my partner and my mom. No one knew the absolute turmoil I was going through internally. I know that many new moms, seasoned moms, any mom, woman, man, dad, etc., go through times in their life and/or parenting journey and struggle just like I did. I now know how common postpartum mental health problems are, but it feels like no one is really speaking out about it. You only see what people want you to see, and no one wants to portray to others that they are struggling — especially over social media (which is where we all get the idea that people have all of their shit together). I am definitely guilty of only sharing the moments on social media that portray a beautiful, happy-all-the-time family life, when in reality no one can be happy all the time! It's impossible!

Many of us (including myself) are so afraid to show what real-life feelings and mental health struggles can do to someone. It's almost like we're all trying to show that we have it all together, living in fear of the stigma that comes when speaking about mental health. **No one wants to look like they don't have it all figured out or that they are having a hard time, but it's impossible to have everything figured out and together all of the time.** We are all human, we all go through hard times, and we all react and deal with hard things differently. We all have a different perspective on every experience. This means that no situation or experience is going to have the same impact on every person. We all feel different ways about the same things. I truly believe life would be so much easier if we all just shared real emotions and real experiences with each other. We'd have fewer people suffering in silence if we all spoke out about what's going on, because we all go through times where we have no f**king clue what we're doing (and that's okay!).

Although this was an incredibly hard time and difficult to admit and get myself to reach out for help, I just want to close off this chapter by letting anyone who reads this know that I am okay now. I sought help through therapy, medication, and self-care. If you are also struggling, please know that seeking help is not always a lifelong ordeal (I thought that once you start, you're required to continue forever). Sometimes you just need help to get through something tough for a short period of time. Try not to be intimidated to contact a therapist. Just write the first email (or make the first phone call)...it will change your life! Put yourself first — you cannot take care of someone else if you cannot take care of yourself. You are important, and your mental health is important. Fight for yourself. You only have one life to live...you deserve to have a happy and enjoyable one.

CHAPTER 15

Rosa Lombardi

PHOTO: **LESLEY BOGAN / PUREAPERTURE**
@ROSIELOMBARDI9

Hi. My name is Rosa. I am simply a woman, a wife to Dino for almost 30 years, and a mother to Diana and Daniel. I am an avid reader, writer, and am extremely sure about one thing: there are many days where I ask myself, *WTF am I even doing?*

It was a Saturday morning. The tunes were blasting Earth, Wind, and Fire's "September" as my husband and I were in the kitchen at the stove making some breakfast. Dino and I were mulling over what we were going to do the rest of this day. It was a perfect day to shop and have a little lunch in some small town. Maybe catch a movie? I turned to plate the eggs, and I stopped short. Standing quietly at the kitchen counter were my kids, Diana and Daniel. Dino stopped pouring coffee to look at me staring at my kids. Seconds go by. Dino and I both turn to each other and ask out loud, "Who are they, and what do they want?" The kids waved and smiled and asked, "What's for breakfast? What are we doing today? Is the family coming over? Can I take the car?" All in a minute, the tunes were changed to some kind of electronic dance music, the breakfast for two suddenly became for four, and reality was terminated by my real-life movie, "They're Back."

Being a mom of 2 adult children is going to be wonderful, they said. You are going to be best friends, they said. There will be fewer arguments, tears, annoyances, and commotion. There will be fewer headaches. They will need you less. They all said it. Less. Less. Less. What does that even mean? *WTF?* I would love to have a chat with those "they said" people right now. Can I just simply say it? Being a mom of two adult children is not easy!

Diana, now 27, and Daniel, 26, left for many years of school and hockey, and I did not take them leaving me at such an early age too well. Like, how dare they? Being their mom was very fulfilling, and I poured it all into being there for them. I knew nothing else for a long time. My time without them was unimaginable. Who would I be without them? However, that very quickly changed, allowing an avenue of full freedom to write and read and go away every weekend and not have to worry about dinners and who needs the car by a certain time. I clearly remember a good friend of mine during my earlier days of sadness without the kids assuring me that they would come back. However, my visions of them coming home were to stay for a bit so we could catch up on life and have them spend quality family time together and settle into their careers, and then bye-bye. BUT THEY ARE STILL HERE.

They moved back in very quickly, with their original belongings and furniture and so much more that they had collected over the years. They filled the house with chatter and laughter and excite ment, but they also filled it with heartbreaks, frustration, junk, and so many laundry loads that my mind and heart are overwhelmed. My feelings are mixed emotions. Moms are supposed to always want their kids around, no? I was elated to have them back, but I was silently not thrilled with all the chaos. Adult kids are more difficult to convince of anything. I do not know what the fuck I am doing or saying some days. I do not have all the solutions or right answers. Our lives and conversations are over-filled with complications of major relationship breakups, questions about careers and options, extremely ill family members, and battling health conditions.

The spiralling was starting. No matter their ages, they still require loads of love and guidance, but at times I was depleted. My mind was racing a mile a minute, and my heart was exploding with angst and confusion over how to protect my kids from the harshness of reality. I had to keep reminding myself they are adults, not 10 and 11-year-olds. I raised them to be independent and kind and to celebrate life. They can handle more than I think. But can I handle what they are handling? As moms, our main fierce mama bear instinct is to protect them, save them, and not let them get hurt, no matter their age. Again, I keep reminding myself that they are adults.

These adult children are harder to ground, too. Their laughter infiltrates my brain when I tell them, "You are both grounded. Get to your rooms." I laugh even to myself. Really? That is all I've got for them? Who grounds adult children? They have not been sent to their room since they were 13 and 14. Quite often, they want your feedback and ask tough questions, but once they hear it, it's "No, Mom, no." If it is not something they want to hear, I get stopped in my tracks with, "Mom, you don't even know what you are saying!" I say yes; they say no. I say black; they say white. I say maybe, they still hear NO. Ugh! So I tell them, "You are adults, figure it out."

Our family of four always has open discussions on everything and anything. But some days, my invisible clipboard is awash. I have no notes, backup plan, or PowerPoint presentation. Some days I have nothing. Can they just go ask or talk with their dad occasionally? He is smart and full of wisdom and clear-cut advice. He lives here too, folks. But, still, the echo of their voices calling "Mom!" bounces off the walls. All of us working from home invites all too easy access to my living room makeshift office. MOM, MOM, MOM. This beckoning was just so I could be shown apparently the funniest TikTok ever made. There is nowhere to hide. It brings me back to when they were 2 and 3, and you could not even pee without one of them looking for you, yelling "Mom!" throughout the house. Even as I am writing this, they are both in the kitchen, one lingering around just making tea and a snack and loudly discussing the weather because the music is cranked at a window-breaking decibel, while the other is vacuuming around me. Can you hear it? I apologize for all the noise. Can a mother just please co-author a book in peace? Or at the very least, can one of them make me a cup of tea? Better yet, pour me a big ass glass of wine.

Throughout the toddler and tween years, I would chant like a mantra: *I can't wait for these two children to be all grown up.* I prayed to gain more patience and sanity, and be able to have a whole adult conversation without a debate and someone walking out of the room and slamming their bedroom door. Let us get one thing straight — I was the door slammer. My mother (R.I.P) had four children and raised and mentored all of us until we were all well into adulthood We all lived at home and did not move out until we were married. I do not know how the hell she did it. There was always a clean house, homemade meals, fresh clean laundry folded AND put all in its place, and hosting family dinners. I do wonder if she ever had these feelings and thoughts of, "When are these kids leaving?"

I wished I had asked her. It could have helped me now in this stage of parenting. I wanted to be my mom's kind of mom. I wanted to be like her. She was always calm and collected and dressed and ready to conquer the moments. I felt like she had it together. Do I have it together? No, but do I really need to have it together? I just put so much pressure on myself to make sure that I am the best version of myself. I love my kids. I love them hard. They are great kids. They work hard and enjoy being around family. Living with them is companionship at its finest, and most of the time it is crazy, fun, and full. But I'm not going to lie, some days living together is difficult. They have their own schedules and habits, and I must remind them that we are not just roommates. For any of you out there reading this, please, please tell me I am not alone? Having some spare and private time would be lovely, and is not having to answer or ask a thousand questions in a week too much of a request?

Rules. It is nice to have rules. Please, I beg them, if you start the laundry, then finish the laundry!! Piles of clean laundry stay in the dryer, on the dryer — there are piles of clean laundry growing everywhere. The dishwasher is empty, but the dishes are in the sink. I just spent a shitload on groceries, but apparently there is no food in the house. Why is every glass I own all around the house? Yes, I know these are small annoyances. But can a mama please, just please, have one clean house for like half a second? I had a taste of life without them for a few years. I had to slow it down and remind myself that it will take time to get used to living with them all over again, and accept the fact that their idea of living together is so much more different than mine. Breathe. It cannot last much longer. Let it go – let it go. I bring up the question very subtly (like once or twice) regarding leaving this house and moving on with their own life, and maybe making me a grandmother or at the very least give me a chance to miss them. Is that bad? Is that selfish of me that I want them to move out and on and away? Unfortunately, they like it here. There is toilet paper, a stocked fridge and pantry, and Netflix. Why would they leave?

I did not always feel this way. My mother warned me that having kids this close in age would create allowances for having them both leave me at the same time. I was convinced at that time that they would be with me forever. I was ok with that. After all, no matter the ages, a parent is a parent is a parent. What I find most difficult is the emotional aspect. Everyone who knows me knows too well that I cry at the drop of a hat. I cried when Diana decided to go away to university. She was moving out. I was so happy for her. But sad for me. My firstborn is leaving me already. Where is the child who screamed for mommy every time I left the room? Exciting times and adventures were upcoming for her. She was the kind of girl to go get what she wanted or needed from the age of two. Her charge and her confidence led her through a weave of life-altering decisions and success. But even with all my anticipation for her, I was dreading what was left for me. My children were growing up and out too fast.

Being a parent is full-time. Every empty second of your day is filled with filling out school forms or driving them to hockey and figure skating and their part-time jobs. It is busy with prepping meals and washing loads and loads of laundry and yelling at them to get ready to be out the door in ten minutes. AND NOW she has the nerve to leave me with a house full of just men — my husband, her brother and our cat Sketcher Bob. Where is my girl power? She is taking it with her to move onto her next chapter of life. I cried for days after we dropped her off. I moped. We talked on the phone, but it was not the same. My life was a little less chaotic, but I wanted to be the 24-hour mom again. I remember someone else telling me "Don't be upset. They do leave. But they always come back — it's not permanent."

Diana never looked back. Her love of school and thirst for knowl edge carried her extremely far in her academics and in challenging herself in all that life threw at her. Knowing she was happy and excelling made me calm and less worried about her. I relaxed and finally fell into my newfound appreciation of more time by spend ing it on myself and my husband and Daniel. Daniel and I had some quality moments to bond together, making life full of a remarkably busy hockey schedule that I was a huge part of and his number one fan.

Suddenly, Daniel decided he was leaving to go play hockey in a town that is 4 hours away and live with a billet family. Well, that did not sit well with me! A billet mom? I am his mom! How could he have another mom? I carried him for more than 9 months (he was late), not her. So, with my mind full of worry and my heart heavy with pain, we dropped him off at this billet house with the new wonderful mom and her family, and I had to say goodbye. I was bawling so hard I could hardly get the goodbye out. My husband tried to console me all the way home and say it was ok and he would be fine. I thought I would not be, though.

I was confident we lost both our kids forever to education and sport and other stand-in moms. I asked my husband, "What if Daniel ends up liking her more as a mom than me?" I worried she would not take care of him the way that I did. You always hear that kids like other kids' moms more. Was this going to happen to me? I cried for weeks. I was a mom without kids at home, and I felt as if I was robbed of more precious time with them. Months later, on Diana and Daniel's first visit back home, I needed them to know how I was feeling. Bless their hearts, I was assured that I was their best mom and that they missed me and home and appreciated us. I was elated that both my kids were flourishing, and that as parents we could let go and I was now prepared to be a parent to adult children. Easy peasy, right?

Yet again, here I write before you all...where is that clipboard, and *WTF am I even doing?*

It was so much simpler when they were 4 and 5. They believed and trusted all that came out of my mouth. In their eyes, I was their supermom who had it all together. I would look at the two of them and think one day, 7 and 8, 15 and 16, now fast forward to 26 and 27. Thinking back, it all seemed easier when they were 4 and 5. They were chatty and witty and full of curiosity and charm. They had their whole lives ahead to dream, learn, and succeed. These little humans are mine, and I helped them come into this world, but shit, am I good enough to be their mother? Most days, hell yeah. Most days, hell no, I do not know how. Motherhood is the hardest role ever. I wanted to quit at times. You might be able to take a fifteen-minute break, but you can't quit.

Each phase was tougher than the next. But as it got tougher, I got kinder with myself. Am I perfect? No, but at 4 and 5, the kids think I am, so I am going to just wing it and protect them and love them as best as I know how. I am still doing that. I wanted to ensure I raised kind, humble, and well-balanced children who would later become well-balanced adults. I wanted them safe, and I wanted to protect their little hearts. All I can do now is be the best version of me. I know how, and I hope that we all understand that the answers really don't have to be perfect. Do other moms have the perfect answer? No! Am I putting such high expectations on myself so that I can still lead them in the right direction? Yes! It's just me over here capeless, trying to do my greatest to guide them through some of their toughest challenges and questions yet. On more than many occasions I have had to bite back my tongue, as we all know that less can be more.

I clearly remember this moment: My son was about 3, and I had him on the washing machine tending to a scrape on his knee. He had those big brown eyes and those long, wet lashes, and the tears were puddled on his plump cheeks. Time stood still. I stared hard at my little man, and my heart burst. All I could think was that someday some girl would break his heart, and I started to bawl right in front of him. He stared back at me. I could barely see him anymore through my tears. I silently promised and pledged to him right then and there that I would be his Mamina forever, and that I would always be there to make sure he knew it. He used to say he was "never going to leave you ever, Mamina," and "I will always live with you and Daddy." I said yes, yes, you will. I did not know that years later, this verbal contract was going to still be ironclad. At age 3, his words were endearing. Today, lol…not so much.

While they were away living their lives, it took me a few months to get into my new groove. I accepted the fact they were gone but not far. We were all enjoying our new paths. I was happy to be a woman again with dreams, a career, and exploring my life and its new challenges without just being referred to as the mom. I started relishing my ample free time. I read more. I shopped alone. I journaled so that I could keep my thoughts and newfound freedom in check. I was starting to get used to my life without being within an earshot of them. Texting and Facetime became our new best friends. They found their independence, and I found mine again. Missing them and seeing them occasionally built our family circle stronger. The little time you spend on the phone or in person on a visit is spent catching up and laughing and hugging. There is no room or time for anything but friendship and love. This is what I, as a mom, envisioned with my children — a relationship built on trust and love and honesty well into their whole life, no matter what stages we are all in. Moms have stages, too!!

Right now, as I reflect on these last few thoughts, the house is incredibly quiet. I look around. My kitchen is clean, there is no loud music or discussion of any urgent matters. It is blissful! I turn to Dino, who reminds me that they'll be back...they're just on a Starbs run.

Big sigh! If all else fails, Dino and I could be the ones moving out.

CHAPTER 16

Sandi Robertson-Brooks

PHOTO: **LAKYN HANN**

@WRITING_WITH_SANDI

The sun will shine
The new day will come
Your heart beats in rhythm
These things are certain

Or are they?
Missed beats
Fast, slow, out of rhythm
Heartbeats can be fixed
A pacemaker for life
To remind your heart of its job

But why? Why?
The lingering question
Unknown the echoing answer
Genetics? Fluke? Birth trauma?
Answers never given

Each stage of life brings new questions
New worries for your heartbeats
Guesses provided but the truth hides
Navigating within the unknowns

Y ou are supposed to be able to count on your heartbeats, right? You are supposed to be able to count on doctors to have the answers. When neither of those are true, all you find yourself thinking is *WTF is going on?*

My name is Sandi, and I have been living for the majority of my life with an incomplete AV block that resulted in me having a pacemaker. That's basically just a really fancy way of saying that sometimes the bottom part of my heart doesn't get the message from the top part to beat. When this happens, my pacemaker sends a shock to get it to beat properly. Now, I am lucky that I use it less than 10% of the time, but that doesn't mean it hasn't affected my life. I am also a mother to my amazing son, and the interaction between pregnancy and my heart condition proved even more interesting than you might think.

My *WTF* moments started before I was even allowed to have that thought while trying to get the diagnosis. As a young girl, I was accused of being an attention seeker when I complained about dizziness. Thankfully, my parents and paediatrician persisted, and we were finally able to get answers, even if those answers were incomplete. My official diagnosis is AV Block, reason unknown. They had no idea what caused the heart issues, and that question has continued to come up since my diagnosis.

Throughout the years, I have fought to have my concerns heard. Scar tissue pain was pushed aside as a side effect and as being exaggerated, only to find out it was one of the worst cases they have ever seen. The questions without answers weighed on me. Anytime that I managed to forget that I had a pacemaker, something would occur that would remind me. Whether it was the heavy feeling in my chest from being too close to strong magnetics or having to avoid going through a metal detector, something would happen. Fun fact: I ended up getting "I have a pacemaker" translated into Spanish so on my trip to Cuba I could communicate properly as to why I could not go through the airport metal detector. Another fun situation was when I went skydiving and had to get a cardiologist to sign off on allowing me to do it — they were quite surprised and said they had not encountered that question before.

Later, the battle over the unknown cause continued, and my cardiologist decided that since I used it so little and we don't know why I had the incomplete block in the first place that I didn't need the pacemaker at all. I tried to voice my concerns when the settings were lowered, and even more so when it was turned off completely. Despite telling the doctor that I was getting lightheaded 20+ times a day, some to the point of struggling to stay balanced, they didn't listen. They actually had the nerve to tell me everyone gets lightheaded, and it wasn't a big deal — like seriously, *WTF?!?* However, what they said was just not sitting right with me.

I knew that something was wrong. Trusting my body and my intuition, I pushed for a test that would show whether the pacemaker needed to be turned back on. Less than 24 hours into a weeklong heart monitoring test, I was getting called to go to the hospital because the pacemaker needed to be turned back on. This just reaffirmed to me that I am the one best able to know what my body is trying to say. Once it was determined that I would continue to need the pacemaker for the rest of my life, our discussions turned to what that meant for my future — specifically what it meant if I wanted to have kids.

Only a small percentage of people who have pacemakers have them as kids or young adults, and when you consider how many of them are female, that doesn't leave very many. This means that there isn't much research or even personal narratives out there of women with pacemakers who have kids. So, at that point, the pacemaker was in my abdomen, and the battery was due for replacement. The doctor and I had to decide whether to just replace the battery or move the pacemaker up to the shoulder. I wanted to know how having a pacemaker in the abdomen would affect pregnancy. The best I got was that it might be a bit more uncomfortable. Ultimately, I chose to move it in part because the idea of having a metal device in my abdomen that could be kicked by a potential baby did not sound fun. Plus, it seemed like most of the limited research and studies available focused on females with pacemakers in their shoulders.

When those two lines appeared on the pregnancy test, I was filled with so many worries and overwhelming excitement, but I must confess the pacemaker was far from my mind. I never considered how much of my pregnancy journey would be decided by my heart diagnosis and the lingering unknown. Like many expecting moms, one of the first decisions I had to make was whether to use a midwife versus an OB. I investigated options and weighed pros and cons, discussed with my husband, asked myself *WTF am I doing?* and ultimately decided to go with a midwife...that was, until I reached out to the midwife only to be told that my pacemaker meant they couldn't take me on as a patient. Suddenly, the choice was taken away from me, and I had to face my mistrust of doctors that had formed from years of not being heard to trust them with my baby.

I made peace with the decision and reached out to an OB who was able to take me on as a patient. We started the journey of ultrasounds, heartbeats, measurements, and discussing family health history. As soon as my pacemaker was mentioned, the additional questions started. They insisted that I see my cardiologist and get his opinion on everything. Reluctantly, I make the appointment to go see him, only to have him tell me that he has no concerns and does not see how me having a pacemaker would affect my delivery. I allowed myself to be optimistic that the question of the pacemaker was behind us and that I could focus solely on all my pregnancy-related questions. However, my OB was not convinced and set me up for a consultation with a high-risk clinic (that I never got the notice about at first, but that is a story for another time). Because of my pacemaker and the unknown reason for the heart condition, it meant they did not know how my heart would handle pregnancy, or, more worrisome, labour and delivery. So, I was then considered a high-risk mom. Now, not only did I have to have an OB, but I would have to deliver at a hospital 45 minutes from home. It seemed like my choices were getting fewer and fewer by the minute.

I could deal with navigating the unknowns for my own health, but then they raised the scary thought of what it could mean for my children. Since we did not know the cause of my heart condition, it meant we did not know if it was hereditary or not. I remember feeling overwhelming worry and guilt at the thought — what if I passed on a heart condition without even knowing? What if my child got it worse than me?

They set me up for my 20-week scan at a specialist clinic with experience with heart conditions. Thankfully, everything came back fine, but the lingering worrying did not stop. I was 8 before symptoms started to present — what if my son was the same? Or, what if my son is fine, but I give it to a future child? The what-ifs kept coming, but the answers were not there to match. The only thing I can be certain of is that I can trust my instincts with my body and my child/ren.

As the pregnancy progressed, the moments of *WTF?* became more frequent. Between the aches, the pains, and the tiredness came the discussion of delivery. As the OBs on my team pointed out, labour and delivery are some of the most intense things that your body can go through, and your body can react in unpredictable ways. While my pacemaker can normally handle any mis-beats that my heart can throw at it, without knowing the cause of the misconnection, we did not know how my heart would handle labour. After reviewing the cardiologist's notes and additional heart tests, they decided to refer me to an anesthesiologist to be prepared in advance if epidural or C-section were needed. After consultation with them, the final recommendation was early epidural to reduce the potential strain and continuous monitoring of my heart. With this decision, my plan for an all-natural birth was taken from me, and I was left wondering where my voice was. These decisions were all being made for me, and my opinion did not seem to matter.

Now I was focused on my plan, but I should have been worried more about what plan my unborn son had in store for us. When he made his decision to come, he wanted to come. I had been feeling off and went to hospital around midnight to be told that my dilation hadn't changed, to go home, and they would see me in two days to be induced. Little did any of us know, I would be back and holding my son less than 12 hours later. By the time we arrived at the hospital, I was already at the point of being ready to push. The nurse asked me why I was high risk and what the plan was. She laughed when I said early epidural, and said that was not happening. Suddenly, I was getting the all-natural birth I had originally hoped for, but without even heart monitoring. This flagged as weird/concerning in my mind, but I was a little too focused on pushing a baby out of me to mention it. Thankfully, we made it through the delivery without my heart doing anything funky, at least as far as we know. The crazy thing is that since COVID lockdown started a week after this and I am low risk/concern, I haven't even had a follow-up pacemaker appointment. So, I guess, more could be revealed.

Now, if I thought the unanswered questions surrounding my health and particularly this pregnancy ended with delivery, I was sorely mistaken. After my son was born, everything seemed perfect, and we were released a little over 24 hours after he was born. However, things started to take a turn 3 days post-birth when the pain and shaking started. I ended up going to the ER only to be admitted to the hospital for 3, almost 4 days. To try to promote rest and due to our concerns with a newborn around the hospital germs at the time, I was admitted to the family unit, but we chose to keep my son at home. Now I was separated from my newborn, and in the worst pain I have ever felt in my life. There seemed to be no end in sight to the pain, but the best the doctors could say was that I had an infection.

Thankfully, strong rounds of antibiotics and pain meds subsided the pain and the infection. Then my questions turned to why. As for that question, they had no answer. In fact, they said that the level of pain I originally felt did not even match what they were seeing. Perhaps that is why the first doctor to see me almost sent me home. Worst of all, they said that since this had happened with my first, there was a chance that this could happen with future children. Some doctors say that, and others say the risk does not change.

Now I am left with even more questions surrounding future children. Will I pass on the heart condition? Can my heart continue to handle it? If I have another, will I end up with another infection or worse? I could choose to let these unknowns be the biggest deciding factor, or I can choose to listen to my heart and my body. Even though all these questions make me say *WTF,* I know that the most significant truths lie within. So, I am willing to embrace all the *WTF* moments that will come along when I choose to grow my family.

One thing that this whole crazy journey has taught me so far is to trust myself. No one knows my body and understands what it might be trying to say better than me. Even when I was wondering what the heck was going on with me. Even when I was wondering what it all meant for me and my baby. Even when wondering why the heck the doctors didn't have answers for me. Even through all that, the one thing I could trust was my own instincts regarding my health. **Sometimes we are just not going to get answers. Sometimes the answers we do get only lead to more questions. So even when thinking "WTF?" your truth and answers are within you to find.**

CHAPTER 17

Sara Easterbrook

@SARA.EASTERBROOK04
SARAEASTERBROOK.COM

5 ...4...3...2...1…Ready or not, here I come! As I slowly tiptoed through my house looking for my adorable two-year-old nephew, I thought to myself as I tripped over books, stubbing my toe on Thomas the Train, getting a whiff of that dirty diaper I just threw out, that maybe, just maybe, having a baby wouldn't be so bad. This part is fun! I pulled back the curtains, ducked under the table, and scoured the basement. This little shit was nowhere to be found. The panic started to creep in. As I ran through my 1300 square foot house shouting his name, wondering where the fuck he could have gone, throwing off duvets, and checking the tub, I thought to myself, *nope, not fucking happening. I'll stick to dogs.* I am in full panic mode now, screaming his name, whipping open the front door, checking the yard. The fear kicks in, and sweat is trickling down my neck. And then…a small giggle. Where is it coming from? I slowly creep up the steps and hear it again. I look in the dog bed, behind the curtain again. As I am walking by the table, I see a little hand. The kid managed to squeeze himself behind the fridge. I pull back the fridge, shaking and furious and happy and sad all at the same time. What the fuck are these emotions? I picked him up, sat him on the step in time out, and I cried like a baby. Me. Not him.

I never had that maternal desire to spawn a bunch of kids. To be honest, I don't even really like kids. I like my nieces and nephews, but that's as far as it goes. They are so busy and sticky. Why are they always sticky? But maybe it's because I was the fucking devil as a child. Or because my mother was killed when I was four. Either way, the maternal instinct was never there. And you know the stories you hear about all the things you did when you were younger? Apparently, I should have had an exorcism with the attitude I had on me. So…the thought of having a mini-me running around out there had me running for the BC pills. You're welcome, world.

I grew up without "unconditional love" or that bond most people have with their mothers. My dad was never one for showing affection or praise. He raised me the best he could with the help of my Godparents. Remember the 90's sitcom *Full House?* That was my life. Yup. My father had the same personality as Danny Tanner just without the hugging. We never went to Disney or on exotic vacations. I grew up in a typical blue-collar family where everyone worked long hours, and we jam-packed life into the weekend. With my father being a single dad and me the first and only kid devil child, and a girl to boot, it was like raising an alien for him. Every June, he would buy me a one-way ticket to Prince Edward Island, where I would spend time with my grandmother for the whole summer. It was the most magical place on earth, filled with wonder and awe. Our sand is red! This was always the highlight of my year! And funny enough, this is now where I currently live with my hubby. Everyone falls in love with our "Gentle Island." It is my favourite place to be, and my heart belongs here. So naturally, we came here for our honeymoon. And 6 months later, we called it home. More on that later.

I loved spending my summers on the "Gentle Island." It was much quieter than the big city of Toronto, and things just went slower. I learned how to play catch off a roof and spent my summers learning T-ball. I was a tomboy. When you are raised by a man, they only really know man stuff. If only you could have seen the panic on his face when Aunt Flo showed up. So I dressed like a boy, always had my hair up, and I even looked like a boy.

One summer morning when I was about 7, I was sitting on gram's living room floor of her 100-year-old farmhouse, the carpet smelling like mothballs and baking soda, sobbing. She told me she was taking me for a haircut and that I was getting a mushroom cut. I didn't want to look like a mushroom. Do you know what mushrooms look like? They look like a penis. Don't ever let anyone talk you into thinking they don't. They do. Thanks, Gram. And everyone was freaking out over the mullet. At least there was always a party going on in the back, and they didn't look like a fucking dick. I still have nightmares about that haircut.

Anyways, I was bullied all through elementary school with the kids asking me if I was a boy or girl. Every day it was "Why are you going into the giiiiirls bathroom?" Kids can be such fucking assholes. You know this. I see your TikToks. So, I played the victim card, and I played it well...we are talking at an Oscar-winning level. I always had an excuse to get out of gym class, track and field, and public speaking. In the end, my Grade 8 teacher told my father that I would be held back if I didn't get my shit together. There was no way I was repeating this nightmare. To say the least, I made it to high school. Kinda.

By this time, my hair had grown out. Thank Yoda. And the braces came off! I was on to my next chapter in life. High school. I will keep this short and sweet. While everyone I went to elementary school with was going to a specific school, I was going to a brand new school where I knew no one. Not one single person. It was a fresh start! I was terrified. I heard all the horror stories of freshmen being stripped of their clothes and tied to the flagpole. What kind of hell was I walking into? It wasn't so bad. It was crowded and loud, and my locker was in the busiest part of the school. It was like stopping on the 401 to let ducks cross the road. It just wasn't going to happen. Be killed or just wait forever. Those were tough choices.

Naturally, being bullied and having no friends for the first 10 years of my life, I made friends with the first person who paid any attention to me. I still remember her coming up to me in the cafeteria. Unfortunately, we didn't remain friends. I wonder what happened to her? I should look her up on Facebook! So, I did what any bullied kid who had no idea how to make friends did — I gravitated to those who spent their time out of the boring classes and under the bridge smoking. Oh ya, I forgot to mention that I tried smoking in Grade 7 and then went all in when I was hanging under the bridge People say pot is the gateway to drugs, but it's not. It's cigarettes.

I spent the first two years of high school being suspended and failing. I had no desire to be there. I was learning things I had no interest in. To this day, I still have never used algebra. They fucking lied! School teaches two things: how to pass tests and how to work for someone else. Nope, not for me. So I dipped when I was 16 Ages 16-24 was a whirlwind of sex, drugs, and alcohol. Look for my next book. You'll hear all about it there.

Eventually, I was sick of working at crappy jobs, barely making any money. It was not something I wanted to do my entire life. So I went to college and got a diploma that gave me the opportunity to niche down and work for crappy jobs that required you to be edu cated, but with benefits. Yay.

People today always tell me how "lucky" I am, how much confidence I have, and how successful I am. Listen, Sharon, I'm successful because I do things that you *won't* do, not that you *can't* do. You just won't even try. I take risks. I take chances. I have no idea *WTF I am doing,* but I do know that if I don't try, I'll be stuck here at some miserable job with Karen, who keeps complaining about Linda and wondering when Felicia is going to peace out. Bye...

And who the fuck wants to live that way? I sure as hell don't. It is bad enough that as I write this chapter, the world is in complete chaos. Adding a shitty job with little pay, no pension, and people who are miserable all the damn time...no thanks. I'll take a chance and risk failing 10,000 times until I get it right. Edison failed 10,000 times, and that one time it worked, and we have light. They make statues of the crazy ones, not the critics!

I heard somewhere that hope is not a plan, and crisis creates breakthroughs. Highlight this shit.

It's not luck. It's not knowing everything. It's not about being perfect. It is NEVER about being perfect, because nothing ever will be perfect. It does not exist. Do you hear me? No matter what you see online, perfectionism is an illusion. Do you want to know the God-honest truth? It is about taking life by the balls and enjoying the ride. It is about falling and getting back up. It's about outgrowing friends. It is about sleepless nights...as I am writing this at 12:30 am. It is about your family judging you and criticizing you for telling YOUR story from your own damn perspective. It is about people thinking you are off your rocker because you don't "clock in" like the rest of the world. And it is so amusing to watch the look on their faces. What do you mean you don't have a job? Where do you get your money? I rob banks. Kidding. I earn it like the rest of you. But when you understand this concept, your mind will be blown. Money comes through your employer, not from your employer. Pow!

I am 37, and I have had 27 different just over broke (job) positions in my lifetime. I lived on autopilot, waking up at the same time on the same side of the bed, doing the same routine in the bathroom. Sitting in traffic on the same routine every day while drinking my coffee from the same hand. Are you as bored as I am?!

Once you get off autopilot and start drinking coffee and masturbating with your other hand, it opens up your world to new possibilities you didn't even know you could experience. It is euphoric. Following the rules doesn't give you pleasure. It's fucking boring and soul-sucking! That is why so many people are just trudging through life — suffering for a paycheck, planning sex, and being addicted to this life of misery and conformity.

My friend, stop vibrating at a low energy and missing out on the pleasures of life, like rocking orgasms in the middle of the day on a Tuesday. Stop planning out your sex! For real, does it make you excited to know that you have planned out your sex? What happened to the good old days of a quickie? And you are never too old to have a midday orgasm. Go out and get some! Now! For real, put the book down and go.

Welcome back! Did you hang onto the bed like you were going to fall off the edge of the earth? Repeat that. Often!

Listen, when I was at rock bottom for the second time, I went from a comfy "secure" — or so I thought — government job to a grocery store clerk. I was $100k in debt and had to tell my husband we had to skip Christmas. It was our first year of marriage...our first year in our new house in our new province with no family, skipping Christmas. When you are that low, you have nowhere else to go but up. So, I took a chance and hired a coach. Tony Robbins says "If you want success, find someone who has the success you want and copy what they do." So I did just that. I paid for a mentor and started a course to self-discovery. It wasn't until I figured out the relationship with myself that everything changed.

I started reading more. I read 27 books in 8 months. I started practicing meditation daily. Now it has become my new norm to meditate 3-4 times a day. I started masterminding with people who spoke the same language as me and were on the same growth mission as me. I started manifesting things into existence. What was once a thought was now my reality. I was able to leave the grocery store and started working with my mentor, helping her to grow her business to over 5 million dollars in the middle of a pandemic. I was creating the most incredible award-winning sales team and meeting new lifelong friends.

The thing about success is you can't do it alone, no matter how hard you try...no matter how much money you are trying to avoid spending. If you want to create a million-dollar lifestyle, you need to surround yourself with the right people. You need to create a vision, and you need to have people on your side who hold that vision with you. When you surround yourself with people with the right mindset, the right attitude, and who love to serve others, you will open up your world to endless possibilities.

Just get out of the way. We tend to stop ourselves from taking chances and experiencing life for fear of the big dreaded F word — Failure! Here's the thing, friend — sometimes we need to take action and learn from our mistakes as we go.

Did you know that our imagination is one of our highest faculties, and it is the reason we have all the results in our life? Think about it. You wake up every morning and think about using the washroom. All of a sudden, you are standing in front of the toilet. Then you think of coffee. BAM, you're now in front of the coffee maker. Then you think about driving to work, and before you know it, you are sitting in your car in traffic on the same route to work. You can create anything that you can imagine. That also includes all the crap you are going through. Are you in debt? Do you keep looking at your bank account and thinking, *when will we ever get out of debt?* This is your imagination showing you the future if you do not get out of debt. And you start fearing *what if we lose the house? What if we can't pay the bills? What if we go hungry?* None of this has even happened in reality, yet you are creating the images in your mind. See how that works?

Now play with me a little here. Pretend you are a 5-year-old and use your imagination. No one needs to hear it but you. What if you were to imagine you had all the money, time, and resources in the world. What would you be? How would you spend your days?

How are you feeling after that? I bet you feel pretty good. You probably even put a smile on your face and forgot all about your astronomical credit card statement. Here's the thing: you can't have a positive and a negative thought at the same time. You also can't think about prosperity and scarcity at the same time. It's one of the natural laws of the universe, the law of polarity. You can't have an up without a down, an in without an out. The same goes for your thoughts. It takes less energy physically and mentally to think a positive thought than a negative one. I didn't understand this until I started studying it.

I suffered from severe depression and anxiety. You wouldn't think so looking at me now. But, before I started studying myself, I had thoughts of death. Often. I kept questioning the point of life. Why did my husband want to be with me? All I did was cry and deny him sex. I spent days in bed, too exhausted to cook or clean or even go out on a date with my husband. I had no desire to do anything. It wasn't until I figured out the relationship with myself that every thing changed.

Once I learned how truly powerful our thoughts are and how they control everything we manifest into the physical, that is when my whole world opened up. My confidence grew. So I attracted more people into my life. Then I became addicted to sharing this feeling and material with those around me. So I read more and learned. I shared what I learned. If you want to earn, you've got to learn — and I don't mean college. That teaches you how to work for someone else. I can teach you how to work for yourself for a fraction of the cost! I became obsessed with the growth of not only myself but those around me. The money was rolling in, and the time freedom was everything I imagined and more! There is no greater feeling than waking up next to your soul mate with no set schedule and fucking pumped to start the day!

Listen, I am 37, and I still have no clue what the fuck I am doing. Am I successful? Yes. But I can tell you this: staying stuck in a job I hated, in a city that made me scared for my life, was not something I wanted to suffer through for the next 70 years. Yes, I plan on living to 107, because let me tell you...regret is scary. No one dying talks about the things they did — they talk about the things they didn't do.

You have to BE what you want. Then you can HAVE it. Leave everyone else out of the equation. It is only you. Trust the process and act as if. It totally fucking works.

CHAPTER 18

Shawna Kressler

PHOTO: **DASHA BALCOM PHOTOGRAPHY**
@COAUTHOR_UNKNOWN

WTF, WTF, WTFFFFFFF!!! These were the words that were running through my head on repeat as we drove to triage for the second time in one day because I was suddenly bleeding for the first time during my first pregnancy at 31 weeks.

If you've had children, chances are you're also now saying "WTF" in your head, because YES!!! EXACTLY!! WTF??!!! "You're supposed to cook for another 9 weeks! I don't have everything I need. My hospital bag isn't packed yet! Your nursery isn't painted yet. Hell, I don't even have a room for you to live in, let alone have it painted!! I'm not ready for you yet, and there is no way that this can be good," is all that I kept hearing on repeat, over and over again.

Hello there! Welcome to my chapter! My name is Shawna Kressler, and this is my story about giving birth at 31+6. For those who don't know, that means my little guy was born at 31 weeks and 6 days. Keeping in mind that full-term is considered 40 weeks, to say he arrived a little early would be an understatement. He was anxious, excited, and ready to take on the world! That or the fact that I had a tear in my placenta, which turned my uterus into a danger zone, and my little genius baby knew that meant it was time to get the fuck out. So out he came at 3lbs, 14ozs, and we began our journey in the NICU.

Talk about a "WTF Am I Doing?" moment. I didn't even know what "NICU" stood for (Neonatal Intensive Care Unit), let alone have any idea what our experience was about to be like. As I was in the triage and the doctors were running through the scenarios of our soon to be decided outcome, they spoke of the NICU, but in no way did I wrap my head around what that experience could be like. And now, coming out on the other side of it, I honestly can't imagine my life without it. So with that, let me tell you a little bit more about it...

In March of 2018, I was 31 weeks pregnant and had been feeling great. I had a fantastic pregnancy...I only felt nauseous once throughout it all, and other than being tired and gaining more weight than desired, all went smoothly...until one day, the spotting started. We went to the triage and they said everything looked fine; it could have been some dried blood, no need to worry. It's great when people tell you things like that, ya know? "No need to worry"...ya, I'd love to not worry, but I know my body and I know something is up, so I'm going to worry a bit, but I'll go home and rest as you suggested. I had an appointment with my OB later in the week, so I figured I'd wait and address my issues with him.

The next day I had some cramping. It was very faint, not alarming but just something I noticed.

I saw my OB the following day and explained how I had been feeling. I told him I had had some faint cramping and some spotting again. He told me to go back to triage and prescribed me a steroid shot. He said that things should be fine, but he'd rather be safe than sorry and advised me of this given where we were at in my pregnancy. If I was to go into labour, the area of concern would be the baby's lungs. The steroid shot was to help boost the lung capacity of the baby. Two injections were needed, 12 hours apart. I left my appointment, headed back to triage (I was becoming a regular there), got the steroid shot, and was told I was 1 cm dilated. Sorry, what? They said that like it was no big deal — like it was the house special that the waiter murmured under his breath. That news hit me like a ton of bricks. They explained that this was normal, that many women dilate around this time in pregnancy and continue to slowly dilate through the remainder of their pregnancy (this was another one of the things I feel that no one really tells you about pregnancy). They said to go home and rest and come back if anything changed. So we went home and ordered some Swiss Chalet. It's funny the details you remember. I remember sitting down for dinner at our dinner table and turning to my husband and saying, "This is going to be our last meal together, I can feel it. We should have splurged on the Keg!" And then I ate all my dinner.

I also sent my husband out to get diapers, diaper cream, baby shampoo, and simple small things that we hadn't really gotten a chance to pack up. I conveniently threw some things in a bag...just in case.

I laid down on the couch and began watching Big Brother (I'm a huge fan) and was greeted with some cramping again, this time a little bit more present than earlier in the week. At first, it didn't really register with me...I had just eaten a full Swiss Chalet dinner (chicken and ribs, if I recall) and was caught up in my show, becoming mindless to the outside world and letting my worries drift away as I sank into my reality TV guilty pleasure. ¾ of the way through, the pains caught my attention as I noticed a bit of a pattern. So I started to time them and, sure enough, I had pains coming every 3-4 minutes. Naturally, I finished the episode of Big Brother, told my husband to grab his things, and off we went back to triage.

We arrived around 10pm, and I was now 3cms dilated. They weren't exactly sure what was going to happen, but they told me at this point that I was going to be admitted into the hospital whether the baby was coming or not, and was going to be bedridden to await their arrival. This was another WTF moment along this journey...I couldn't understand how I was just suddenly at the hospital and not leaving until the baby was born, given that I still had 8 weeks until I was full-term. My mind was swirling about work, we had bought a house that we needed to move into, there was still so much to do, and it all didn't make sense to me. It was a sudden shift, full of uncertainty and worry.

So I was moved down to the maternity ward as they had a vacancy, and they weren't yet certain of my outcome. I started to experience more and more cramping...contractions, we can now call them. However, I still wasn't convinced at the time, so they administered morphine, which just made me sick. They said to try and rest, and the contractions continued through the night. I had been continuing to dilate, but very slowly. At 6am, the doctor came in to see me as it was time for the second dose of my steroid shot. They went down to check me out and advised that I was at 10 cms and that it was time to push.

We went from not being sure if the baby was coming, being told to just rest, to now fully being asked to push and get the show on the road. I asked for an epidural. I was able to get that and then was put on standby as my doctor had to deal with an emergency C-section.

Back he came, and off we went. I pushed for about 15 minutes, and they were about to vacuum my babe out when I thought, *He must be a peanut...most women can push out watermelons, you can do this!!* and then I pushed out my little baby boy.

We didn't know the sex beforehand, so I hear "He has balls" from my husband, learning that I had just become a Boy Mom.

I was told I wouldn't get skin to skin time as they would have to rush him down to the NICU to make sure everything was ok, but he came out crying and peed on the doctor, which they thought was great...so I got that first cuddle somewhat unexpectedly, and then, in the blink of an eye, off he went.

The next 24 hours were a blur. Thankfully, our son's health was stable and not in any sort of serious danger from an early delivery. We learned that he had to develop his eating skills, and would have to put on weight before leaving. Other than jaundice, some bruising from birth, and a feeding tube, he was healthy, and we were over the moon thankful for our new, earlier than expected little gift. From our family and friends shocked by the news, pouring in to see us, to trying to learn the restrictions and rules of the NICU, and not to mention navigating this new postpartum world, everything was moving a mile a minute and we were riding this weird kind of high.

One of the nurses came in and told me it was time to learn how to pump. She said that since he came early, chances are my milk wasn't in yet, but we would work on getting out some colostrum, a.k.a. Liquid Gold. She rolled in this archaic-looking machine, which was one of the hospital breast pumps. That thing just looked scary, and sounded even scarier once it was turned on! At this point, I hadn't really thought much about breastfeeding. I knew I was going to try for it but was willing to accept whatever outcome we would have. But I guess I never really thought through the process. I KNOW I didn't think through the process.

After a few minutes of being hooked up to the pump for the first time, the nurse unwrapped an empty syringe and showed me how to massage around my areolas to gently apply pressure, which results in your ducts "pussing" out that Liquid Gold. It sounds gross, but it's so satisfying to get some out. It's harder, though, to then try and suck it up into the syringe. I thought that this was crazy and didn't understand why we were doing this. It seemed like such a small amount, and there was no way it was impactful. Boy, was I wrong! That stuff is PACKED with nutrients! It's so, so good for the baby, so I instantly turned it into a competition between my two girls to see who could produce more for our little guy! For those interested, my left side won.

It came time for me to get discharged and for us to leave the hospital, which meant leaving our little man for the first night. I knew this moment was coming, and I knew that I could handle it. We were already so grateful to the staff in our NICU. I knew he was safe and in good hands, and we had things to do. I had to go out and purchase a new double breast pump, as advised by the lactation consultant, and was looking forward to sleeping in my own bed. Well, of course, none of that went as planned, and I was a mess. I was sobbing over the isolette and felt like the worst mother known to man. How could I leave him? How could I just go home and continue on while he was there? For those of you who know this moment, you're my inspiration, as I wouldn't wish this on anyone.

Once my milk came in, I switched from using the hospital pumps to my own, which I had received as a gift from my shower. Mommas to be, I'm going to tell you something VERY important right now so please read this and remember it: ALWAYS SPLURGE ON THE DOUBLE BREAST PUMP. It's something I wish someone had said to me, as I didn't know the difference. We were at home; it was the morning after we had been discharged. I was sitting on the couch with a cup of tea, and I started up the single pump. I didn't think much of it; everything seemed to be working fine, I wasn't in pain…when all of a sudden my other breast started shooting out milk EVERYWHERE!!! WTF? What was happening? What was I doing wrong??? I yelled at my husband to grab a bowl to catch it all! We knew at this point how important my milk was for our son, and we didn't want to miss a drop. This led to me having a total meltdown. Right away felt like a failure of a mother. Isn't it crazy how hard us mothers are on ourselves? I was a first-time mom and I had NO IDEA, but we never allow ourselves that grace. I was mad, angry at myself for not knowing better, angry at my husband for not using this as an opportunity to audition for the Toronto Blue Jays by showing off some amazing catching skills, and I felt like I let my son down. Oh, the guilt. As mothers, we'll carry it forever.

The next day, we began a new routine that lasted for the next 34 days. We spent 12 hour days in our new home away from home. My husband was able to take a couple of days of his paternity leave, but we wanted to be mindful of saving some time for when we would eventually be at home, so it soon became a solo mission for this momma.

The NICU turned into this safe haven for me, and the nurses became my family, my friends, and my closest allies. They taught us how to give our son a bath, different feeding techniques, how to change him, and how to hold him. Without this team of people, I'm not sure I would have figured it out. As crazy as it sounds, I was scared to hold him...he was so small. And I'd ask if I could hold him, ask if I could do the next diaper change...why was I asking? He was mine!!! But I didn't know how this all worked, and they helped me through every step of the way (Karen and Dawn, I hope you have the chance to read this to know how much you mean to us, how much you helped us, how much we admire you, and how we honestly don't know how we've done it without you up to this point!).

As much as it was a safe haven, it was also scary as hell. Tubes, machines, beeps, and longer beeps filled the room. We learned how to read his oxygen levels, his heart rate, and we would even know how much he would get from each feed. We were spoiled with information. Once we left, this part was a huge adjustment because we no longer knew. We no longer knew if his heart rate was where it should be, if his oxygen levels were fine. We didn't have the same scales and couldn't figure out how much he was getting from each feed, if he was even fed at all...it's great to know all of the information in the moment. Still, man, is it hard to not rely on those facts to know everything is fine once you're out in the real world.

I knew that I wasn't prepared to take on this new journey that was motherhood. I still had so many questions and was unsure of so many things. I was hoping to get some clarity as to what to expect when we did our prenatal birthing class. I'm sure we would have, had we made it. Ironically, we were scheduled to take it the weekend my son was born...because of course we were!

Looking back now, I can't even imagine what our experience would have been like without the NICU. It hit me on that last day. The day my son was discharged was such a day full of emotion. For starters, it was our first wedding anniversary. We had just bought a new house and spent the last week moving in and getting ready, anticipating that our little guy would be joining us soon (that's a chapter in itself talking about the guilt you have when you're not at the NICU every waking moment of your day!). Apart from scheduled deliveries, many parents don't know when their last night as a twosome will be. We knew when we left the hospital on May 4th that we were bringing our little boy home the next day. The nurses in the NICU encouraged us to go out for dinner, have a few glasses of wine, and sleep, as this was a special moment for us, getting ready to embark on this new journey the next day. As much as we wanted to, we stayed at the NICU till our usual time, came home to the new house, and worked to finish the nursery till the wee hours of the morning.

I now wished we would have done the dinner and wine. He didn't even sleep in his nursery until he was 3 months old. ALWAYS DO

THE WINE!!! It's one of the only things I didn't listen to the NICU nurses about, and they were right.

When we arrived back at the NICU on our final day, there was a buzz in the air. You were always so happy for the parents and babies who were graduating out into the real world. We had dressed up in more than our usual sweats, the sun was shining, and our little guy had had a great night prior to our morning arrival.

We spent the morning there as we normally would, going through a lot of the same motions we had for the last few weeks. We gave him a bath, we did a few feedings, and chatted with the nurses while he slept...and then it came time to leave.

Leave?? I suddenly couldn't leave. I didn't know what the fuck to do once I walked through those doors with this baby. He had never been outside the NICU, let alone in an elevator, car, or around other people with their germs (and to think this was pre-COVID-19). I was freaking out and didn't want to go. We knew we wouldn't have access to the same kind of information at home, and how would we know that everything was fine? **I couldn't fathom the fact that I was about to walk out there and was expected to mother and just know what to do.** *WHAT THE FUCK AM I EVEN DOING????* is all I could think as I finally walked out those doors. My mind was a blur. I was crying, hanging off our primary nurses who had become my second mothers, my best friends, my confidants, my leaders, my counsellors, my guides, and my faith. It was because of them that my little boy was able to leave that day. It was because of them I knew how to change a diaper and give him a bath. It was because of them I knew how to pump milk, use a nipple shield, and different latch techniques...and the idea of doing any of it without them was the most terrifying thought I ever had.

All these thoughts then made me realize that this is motherhood. For those who don't experience the NICU and go full-term or longer, you birth your babe and then you leave the hospital — sometimes less than 24 hours afterwards — and embark on your motherhood journey, with no clue what you're doing or how to do it. And here I am, now almost feeling spoiled for having had this experience, meeting these passionate caregivers who made my baby's health their number one priority, and reflecting differently on a place that most parents never want to experience.

It's made me thankful for my time there, as I'm not sure how I would have navigated postpartum without it. It impacted me so much that I have now joined the hospital volunteer board as a Family Advisor for the NICU. It's a small way to give back to something that has been so impactful on my life. The team that was there will never know the impact they make on NICU parents. The compassion they show, the patience they have, the way they leave their troubles at the door and make you and your baby the focus of their attention the whole time they are there...they are so special, in ways I'll never be able to truly describe.

I've never stopped thinking, WTF am I doing? I'm a mother...we think it every day, with every decision we make. That's motherhood in a nutshell.

But never did I think I'd go through such a WTF experience navigating the NICU and come out on the other side being as thankful, respective, and reflective as I am of my experience there. I know myself and my family are the lucky ones, and not everyone's NICU experience is as endearing as ours was. There is something to be said about finding beauty in catastrophe, comfort in despair, and calm amongst the chaos, and that is what the NICU was for us. As the NICU becomes something of our past, it is somewhere that will live on in our hearts forever.

When we're little girls dreaming about what our lives will be like when we're older, we don't dream of all the complications that life can throw our way. Instead, our dreams are so pure and innocent, full of joy and wonder. But don't be fooled. Those same little girls are strong and determined, willing and able. We are made for the unknown, and we will always rise to the occasion — because life is really just a whole lot of *What the Fuck* moments. It all comes down to how you choose to handle them.

CHAPTER 19

Tesha Gibbon

PHOTO: **LEAH SMITH BRANDING**
@SIMPLY_OVERCOME

❝ Don't make the same mistakes I did."

That more or less sums up all of the motherly advice I ever received from my own mother. Now, don't get me wrong…there were other tidbits of advice scattered throughout my childhood, but this was the overriding theme. My mother did not want me to follow in her footsteps.

I understood from a young age that my mother expected me to break the cycle of poverty and abuse and to rise above the circumstances of my birth and upbringing. You see, I was born to a 17-year-old mother and a not much older father who didn't stick around long enough for me to have any memory of him — making me, essentially, the third generation of fatherless daughters.

Until I was 11 years old, we lived in a concrete jungle, surrounded by poverty, where any extras we had were a result of the generosity of my grandmother and step-grandfather. From there on out, we just kept moving. By the time I was 18 years old, I would guess that we had moved approximately 15 times. I say approximately because the moves were so frequent and so abrupt that I just don't trust my ability to accurately remember them all.

To put it mildly, things were not easy. There was love and magic moments, but little of the consistency or stability that a child needs, and more than my fair share of trauma. I saw my mother grow up, try to find love, and build a better life for us. I watched her fight to find her footing in a world hellbent on knocking her down, just as she had watched her own mother do. I stood helplessly as she entered and left an abusive relationship repeatedly. I watched her struggle to start over again, with literally nothing but the garbage bags filled with stuff that we had managed to pack as we escaped. I witnessed life knock my mother down over and over again, but I also witnessed her pick herself back up over and over again.

My first few years of high school were a bit of a roller coaster Sometimes I did well enough to pass my classes, but other times frankly, I did not. In fact, I repeated all of the ninth grade due to my complete disinterest in attending school at all. I was what they called a "chronic non-attender." The Vice Principal at the high school told my mother that he didn't expect I would ever graduate and given the path I was on at the time, he was probably right to have said so. I had a whole shit load of stuff going on to contend with, and school was simply not my priority.

I distinctly remember sitting in an eleventh grade English class when my teacher gave the class a lecture. He said, "Shit or get off the pot!" I had never heard that expression before, nor had I ever heard a teacher cuss, and I was hooked. The gist of the lecture was this: "It is time for you to shit or get off the pot. If you want to get into university, now is the time to start acting like it. If you aren't willing to put in the effort, somebody else will. There are only so many spots. So if you want a spot, do what you came here to do." Now, I doubt that the lecture was specifically directed at me, but it resonated with me on a deep, life-changing level. It felt as though he was speaking right at me, and in my heart, I knew he was right. From that point forward, "Shit or get off the pot" would be my motto.

I knew there was a better life out there for me, and I wanted it. I knew that I had to take control of my own destiny. I knew that, ultimately, what I did or didn't make out of my life rested solely on my shoulders. Nobody was coming to save me. My 16-year-old self had it all figured out. I knew exactly what to do, so I made a life plan...

1. Don't get knocked up

2. Get into university

2. Graduate

3. Start a career

4. Marry a good man

5. Become a mom

Once I had made up my mind, there was no stopping me. I changed high schools (as the result of yet another move), and named my twelfth-grade year my "Shit or Get Off the Pot Year." This was my fresh start, a chance for me to reinvent myself. I never missed a class. I always did my homework. I actually studied. I started to get good grades. I made the honour roll. Surrounded by family chaos, domestic violence, and alcohol abuse, I just put my nose down, and I got my own shit together while the walls around me crumbled.

And guess what? It worked. I got into the university program of my choice. Then, for 4 years, I took public transit 1.5 hours each way every weekday, using stolen bus tickets to pay my fare. I attended just about every lecture. I studied (long public transit rides lend themselves well to that end) and always worked a part-time job (or two) to help pay for it. I managed to graduate with a degree, still owing $20,000 in government student loans. I also managed to be the first woman in my family to get a post-secondary degree.

After I finished university, I hustled, working as many as three jobs at a time, trying to keep up with paying for rent, food, transportation, and all of that student debt. Hustling was the only thing that I knew I could do to improve my socio-economic position and create some sense of stability. That's all I really wanted — stability. A stable relationship, a stable job, and a stable home.

Eventually, I met a wonderful man, who I knew without any doubt would be a good husband and father. As somebody without a father of her own, I was determined not to have my children suffer the same fate. As a young woman, I had vowed that I would love my future children enough to find them a good father (unlike my own) and that is exactly what I did. We bought a house, we got married and we started a family.

When I had my first daughter, it was love at first sight. I mean, the absolute deepest, purest love I'd ever felt. I recognize that this isn't the experience for many new mothers, but it was mine. I loved that little baby with every fibre of my being from the moment I laid eyes on her. I was a mom now, and I was hell-bent on doing right by her

In other words…I did it. I accomplished everything I set out to do I was living my dream. My deepest heart's desire was that I would settle down and live in a regular house in a regular neighbourhood where my kids would have two loving parents. I wanted a normal life, and I was doing the damn thing. I was breaking the cycle.

was not making my mother's mistakes.

So here I was now, fulfilling my life's dreams, and yet, I still didn't feel quite settled. **Now that I had "made it," I wasn't sure what the fuck I was supposed to do next.** I'd never really considered getting any further than this point. I'd more or less been in survival mode for so long, just trying to get through life, that I never really considered what I would do once I got there.

There seems to be this thing that happens when we reach our goals where we forget to stop and revel in our accomplishments, and we just start setting new goals. So now, it wasn't enough that I had stability. I wanted a bigger home...filled with all the things. I wanted a newer car, nicer clothes...and so on. I didn't just want to be some ordinary mom, I wanted to be the "Perfect Mom." I wasn't going to settle for any "B" on the imaginary "Mom Report Card." — my goal was "A+."

I had this vision in my mind of the perfect mother. Let's call her "Hannah." Hannah is basically a 50s television mom who also has a successful career outside of the home. She is always dressed pristinely, with her hair, makeup, and nails done. Her home is spotlessly clean. She is kind, generous, and patient. Her children are clean, perfectly polite, and well-behaved. Hannah is completely self-sacrificing, and would do anything for her family. She's also the type that gets shit done. Hannah is respected at work and in her community. She does yoga every morning. She exercises every day. She sews, irons, cooks, and bakes. She is ever-present whenever her children, husband, or friends need her. Her children confide in her, and the neighbourhood kids adore her. She is the picture of love, calm, and grace. I could keep going, but I'll spare you. The point is that I had this unreasonable standard that I was trying to achieve.

Let me tell you: during that first year of parenthood, I was a martyr - the picture-perfect first-time mother (if by picture-perfect you think of unwashed hair and breastmilk stained shirts). I was ever-atten-tive, ever-present, and solely dedicated to my daughter, Matilda's, well-being. I was going to do all of the things that I had heard were good for babies. I went to baby yoga, baby swim, baby music, baby sign language, and baby massage classes. I spent countless hours sitting on the floor playing with her, singing to her, holding her, and letting her climb all over me. I tended to her every need and whim. I cared for and doted over that baby like "good moms" do. I had this thing in the bag. I was a mother now, and that's all that mattered.

The person I was before motherhood sort of just ceased to exist. I did nothing for myself. I didn't pamper myself, or see friends, or read books, or go anywhere without the baby. I did not partake in any sort of self-care, because I thought this was what good moms were supposed to do. Good moms didn't need to do anything for themselves. Good moms were wholly satisfied just being moms.

Then it came time for me to return to the workforce, and sudden-ly that confidence I had in motherhood began to wane, and fast. I wanted to be both a good mother and a good teacher, but I didn't know how to have both of those things exist without competing against one another. I'd feel guilty if I worked late. I'd feel guilty if I didn't put in extra hours at work. I really struggled to strike that sweet spot. I didn't feel like I could give to both equally at the same time. It felt like I was half-assing both work and motherhood. The elusive work-life balance seemed just out of reach.

Then, we had another baby girl named Adelaide, and my journey to becoming "Hannah" got a whole lot harder. I truly felt that my daughters deserved that perfect mom, but having two young chil dren, working full-time, and wanting to be so perfect all of the time was exhausting and overwhelming. I so desperately wanted to be Hannah, but I just wasn't, and I felt like a failure.

I didn't know exactly what I was doing wrong, but I was struggling to keep it all going. I'd spent years trying to bring this imagined little life into reality. I'd worked my tail off and hustled, afraid that if I eased up on the gas for even a second, it'd all come crashing down on me. I actually had no clue what I was supposed to be doing. I worked full-time, sat on the parent council, planned elaborate outings and birthday parties, had the latest, greatest toys and baby gear, renovated my house, and had a side hustle. I said "yes" to everybody. I was so busy that I couldn't even think straight. I was irritable. I was forgetful. I couldn't keep track of all the things I thought I was supposed to do, despite my elaborate list-making. The daily grind was leaving me utterly depleted.

My self-worth became wrapped up in this vision of "Hannah, the Perfect Mother" that I had in my mind. I would see all of these other moms and think to myself, "Why can't I have it all together like her? How does she always look so put together? How does she keep her house so spotless? I bet her kids are never late for school. I bet she always returns the library books on time. I bet she always..." And that comparison game went on and on. Why couldn't I just be more like them? Am I not enough? Am I too damaged? Do I not deserve to be here after all? In my mind, everybody else had their shit together, and I was the only one just keeping my head above water.

Here I was, living the dream, in a safe community, and belonging to a socio-economic class that wasn't like the one I'd grown up in. Now that I was here, I felt like a fraud. I'd been thrust into this world of motherhood, and my social circle shifted to include other moms that I met in my community. I was surrounded (or at least I thought) by Hannahs. They were women who grew up in one house, with two loving parents and family vacations. They were people who'd had parents that helped pay for their education, weddings, and down payments on their first homes. With their pumpkin spice lattes, high-end yoga wear, and salon hairstyles, they talked about spa days and brand names, and frankly, they spoke a language that I just didn't understand. I had made it, but I did not feel like I fit in here.

Then, one day when Adelaide was 3 and Matilda was 5, I sat with my husband in my doctor's office and listened as the doctor said, "So it looks like cancer..." and just like that, I became a cancer patient. I felt like the rug had just been pulled out from under me. I had finally found stability, and then life threw this at me? How could I have been so naive to think that catastrophe wasn't just around the corner? Of course it was. It was always just lurking there.

Internally, I was falling apart. I couldn't eat, I couldn't sleep, I couldn't focus, and I couldn't sit still. I had panic attacks. I was a wreck, but most people would never have guessed. Externally, I kept up the facade. I kept doing all of the things. I took the kids to extracurricular activities, made money on the side, volunteered at the school, and hosted playdates, all while undergoing test after test and attending appointment after appointment. I still really felt so much pressure to be everything to everybody and keep a smile on my face while doing it.

As part of my treatment, I would have to have a full hysterectomy, which brought with it the inability to have more children, a month-long recovery, and a year of pelvic floor physiotherapy. Then it was just over. That was it. It was over. I was medically well, but mentally I was in a very dark place.

For a long time, I struggled to even accept that I was physically well, like deep down I was holding on to the cancer. I just couldn't let it go. I couldn't release all that fear, sadness, and anger I'd been keeping in. I finally fell apart. I sobbed uncontrollably. I was angry, withdrawn, and unable to organize my thoughts. I was having nightmares. I was having flashbacks. I was having anxiety attacks. I startled easily. I was scared shitless all of the time. Turns out I had PTSD.

As I began to put the pieces of my post-cancer life back together

I went through a period of intense self-reflection, wherein I really asked myself, *What the fuck am I even doing?* I knew that I couldn't ever go back to the way things were. I didn't want to feel like a hamster on a wheel anymore. I didn't want to keep hustling. I'd worked my butt off to get to where I was, but I never eased up on the gas long enough to take it all in. I had broken the cycle. Like, I actually did it. I'd made it. I fucking made it! And I never stopped once to actually let that sink in, and just be happy or proud of myself.

I'd expended so much energy trying to live up to these impossible expectations and then beating myself up for not meeting them. I wore "busy" like it was a badge of honour. I'd spent 5 years trying to pretend that I was the mom who had it all together, while on the inside I had no clue what I was doing, and I hated myself for it. I just knew that this was not the way I wanted to live my life anymore.

I sat down and asked myself, *What do YOU actually think a good mother is? Not a perfect mother, but a good mother? What are YOUR values?* I had no clue what I actually believed deep down. I'd been treading water for so long, just trying not to drown. I'd neglected to actually consider my own values and beliefs.

Figuring out what I actually thought wasn't a simple task either. My own values had become so entangled with what others had told me to believe, I had forgotten how to even think for myself. So I wrote all of my beliefs down, and just stared at them…there were a lot, and many of them conflicted with each other. No wonder I didn't know what the fuck I was even doing. I literally had no clue, no road map, and no real-life person to model motherhood after. I was clueless.

The more that I looked at that list, the more I realized that it was impossible to be all of those things at once. **Nothing was wrong with me, but something was wrong with the expectations.** I had bought into the societal ideal of motherhood. In truth, my upbringing meant that my emotional needs were not always met. TV shows left me dreaming of the type of family I wanted to have. Visits to friends' homes left me yearning for a more wholesome home life. I based my image of the "perfect mother" upon little snippets I observed, because I didn't have much else to go on. I picked up all these little messages throughout my life about what made a good woman. On the one hand, of course, I knew television wasn't real and that TV moms weren't real, but it had still somehow become ingrained in me that it was the standard I should be relentlessly pursuing.

All of this self-reflection led me to a dramatic shift in mindset and lifestyle. I stopped putting everybody else before myself. I stopped saying yes all the time. I stopped trying to be perfect. I stopped shopping to make myself feel better. I got rid of about 50% of my physical possessions. I invested in self-care. I started reading for pleasure. I started writing. I started making time to do things for myself, like painting my nails or watching tv. I began practicing gratitude. I started talking more openly about my struggles. I started giving myself the compassion I'd only previously reserved for others.

I finally figured it out. Nobody actually knows what they are doing. Nobody. None of us. Not a single one. My mother didn't know what she was doing. I don't know what I'm doing. All of those women that I used to envy and compare myself to, they don't have a fucking clue either. We all have our own stories. We're all just trying our best. Even if we make it look as though we have it figured out, we don't. None of us knows what the fuck we are doing You're not the only one.

Other books available from

P U B L I S H I N G

For more information on books, publishing and co-authoring, visit

L E A D - H E R . C O M

Manufactured by Amazon.ca
Bolton, ON